Michael Solomon has done it again. He lines up Marketing's sacred cows, and then he methodically tips over each one. This incisive guide to today's consumer gives us the vision we need to create products and services that will resonate with these new chameleons.

— *PHILIP KOTLER*

Marketers, TEAR DOWN These Walls!

Liberating the Postmodern Consumer

MICHAEL SOLOMON

To Gail – There are no walls between us.

© Michael Solomon 2018

Print ISBN: 978-1-54392-344-5

ebook ISBN: 978-1-54392-345-2

All rights reserved. This book or any portion thereof may not be reproduced or used in any manner whatsoever without the express written permission of the publisher except for the use of brief quotations in a book review.

CONTENTS

Preface xv
About the Author xix
Other Books by Michael Solomon xxi
Think Out of the Box. Your Customers Are! 1
    A Chinese curse decrees, "May you live in interesting times." 2
    The Truth is Out There 4
    Apples to Apples 6
    Apples, Oranges … and Throw in Some Strawberries: Market
    Disruptions Destroy Categories! 8
    The Omnichannel Consumer 10

Wall #1: Us vs. Them 15
    Young Vs. Old 16
    Black vs. White 22

Wall #2: Me vs. We 25
    The Old School, Linear Model of Consumer Decision Making 27
    Today's Nonlinear Consumer Decision Making:
    Who Moved My ZMOT? 29
    The Rise of the Hive Mind 40
    The Hive Mind Makes Honey – and Money: Why Marketers
    Should Care 44
    The Hive Still Needs Queen Bees: We Call Them Curators 49

Wall #3: Offline vs. Online 59
    From Offline to Online 62
    From Online to Offline 75
    The Merger of Offline and Online: Another Wall Down 78
    Product Development 81

Wall #4: Producer vs. Consumer 81
    Advertising and PR 87
    Distribution and Retailing 96

Wall #5: Male vs. Female 101
Androgyny: The Best of Both Worlds? 103
The End of Gender Binarism? 107

Wall #6: Work vs. Play 111
Work Becomes Play 112
Play Becomes Work 114

Wall #7: Body vs. Belongings 121
You Are What You Buy 122
You Buy What You Are 130
This Wall is Down! What's Next? 133

Afterword: Then vs. Now 137
Rich Vs. Poor 138
Right Vs. Left 140

Endnotes 143

WHAT PEOPLE ARE SAYING ABOUT
Marketers, Tear Down These Walls!!

Solomon makes a compelling case for more enlightened marketing in a post-modern world. He shows that simply adapting to the latest consumer trends or fads is no longer enough—something more fundamental is afoot. Use these insights to build a better strategy for your business!

John Wittenbraker, Ph.D.

Global Director, New Business Development, GfK

Solomon has produced an easy read for a marketing text and a long overdue challenge to traditional marketing practice. He candidly illustrates, with up to date data and examples, how first world consumers are changing their habits and shifting their patterns of consumption in response to the hyperconnected digital world and "mega" trends, such as mobile; AI and robotics. The key to understanding the rich opportunities that now manifest for marketing "peeps," he reckons, is qualitative research and a "giga" shift in thinking.

Dr. Tarlok Teji

former Partner & Head of Retail at Deloitte and Visiting Teaching Fellow at Manchester Business School.

Solomon leads the reader on an insightful journey and timely analysis of the post modern consumer that is packed with history, data, and unmatched experience. Whether you are an aspiring entrepreneur, running a small business or an established leader in any emerging field, this book is a must-read. Solomon successfully redefines and decodes the modern consumer as it's never been done before, setting his readers on the right path to win.

Rocco Cardinale

VP Marketing, Franklin Foods (U.S. Subsidiary, Hochland SE of Germany)

As a serial direct marketer for over 35 years, and a lifelong student of the craft, I look for books (and voices) who are taking everything we have learned up until now and turning it all on its head for deeper understanding. Michael Solomon is one of those voices, re-equipping us with new tools and ways of thinking to deal with an unknown marketplace of the future…but a marketplace that is the most exciting than we ever could have imagined. His latest work debunks many of marketing's sacred cows with the goal of taking us to places no one has taken us before. His experience as one of the world's experts in consumer behavior qualifies him to take us to this place, a place where he can make sure we are ready for what's coming. This is a must read for every marketer (or anyone) who wants to be relevant offering products and services based on what consumers demand today (and will demand even more tomorrow)—and as those consumers change their needs and wants in a shorter time frame than ever before.

Brian Kurtz

Titans Marketing LLC, Former business builder of Boardroom Inc. and author of *The Advertising Solution*

Solomon is a marketing maverick who compels you to alter the way you think about your customer, your competition and the not-so-neatly defined world around you. Everything you thought you knew about marketing will make sense in a completely different context as you look through Solomon's lens.

>Kimberly Richmond
>Principal, richmondmarketing+communications

Get ready to take a sledgehammer to your old way of thinking about marketing and consumers. Michael Solomon's newest book turns old school ideas on their head and helps you see marketing —*and the consumers you're marketing to* — in an entirely new light. This is a must read book for anyone who wants to stay up-to-date on the latest developments in the business.

>Jamie Turner, author, speaker, and CEO of 60SecondMarketer.com

Solomon's *Tear Down These Walls!* is a brilliant read with the eye-opening power of *Thinking Fast and Slow* applied to marketing. Solomon challenges marketers to step away from neat and tidy methods of target segmentation in a revealing and accessible way. He provides language that reflects the reality of the post-advertising, multi-channel, hyper-fragmented, insert-buzzword-here environment that businesses need to navigate for success. Most importantly, it shows the way to think about communicating with people, not marketing to "consumers" reduced to percentages in cross-tab cells.

>Sara Bamossy
>Chief Strategy Officer, Pitch

PREFACE

We change our identities faster than a chameleon changes color. On Monday, you may be a Hugo Boss suit-wearing salaryman who listens to Adele, reads *The Wall Street Journal*, quaffs a greasy burger for lunch, and tunes in to *Fox News*. Come Saturday, out come the tats from underneath the starched collar, you ditch the suit for a Kid Dangerous tee and Vans kicks, you down a tuna poké with a craft beer, and listen to Imagine Dragons while you check out the latest issue of *High Times*.

Just what lifestyle category do you belong to? Good luck to the marketer who tries to describe you. Today's *postmodern consumer* defies categorization – sometimes deliberately. S/he yearns to be liberated from cubicles, labels, "market segments," and especially those confining walls that restrict him or her from expressing the unique self that's constructed out of all the lifestyle "raw materials" that marketers of many stripes have to offer.

The postmodern revolution requires marketers to revisit the walls they've erected over many years. That's not an easy thing to do. Conventional marketing strategies are built upon predictability, stability and the comfort in knowing that we can "understand" our customer yesterday, today and tomorrow. We love to wall off people into categories, and often into superneat dichotomies – and call it a day. Those walls used to be solid, and marketers relied upon them to build a structure that formed the basis of their traditional strategic worldview. But now many of these walls are crumbling – and fast. They are like safety hazards that threaten successful brands from thriving in the postmodern revolution. And, they obstruct our view of the marketing possibilities that lie beyond them.

In this book, I'll describe many familiar walls that form the bedrock of marketing strategy and thought today. Then I'll demolish them. I'm going to talk about seven really BIG walls (in **bold** below), but in the process I'll also deal with a lot of other ones. Here are the walls that no longer exist, in convenient alphabetical order:

Arts vs. Crafts

Black vs. White

Body vs. Belongings

Editorial vs. Commercial

Elite vs. the masses

Fake vs. Authentic

Friend vs. Stranger

High art vs. Low art

Home vs. Office

Humans vs. Computers

In here vs. Out there

Kids vs. Teens

Male vs. Female

Me vs. Them

Me vs. We

Offline vs. Online

Old vs. Mature

Owning vs. Leasing

Parent vs. Friend

Producer vs. Consumer

Reality vs. Fantasy

Reality vs. Mythology

Retailers vs. Customers

Sacred vs. Profane

Service providers vs. Consumers

Then vs. Now

Us vs. Them

Work vs. Play

Young vs. Old

I hope you enjoy reading about these walls as much as I enjoyed knocking them down.

Michael R. Solomon

Philadelphia, PA

January 2018

ABOUT THE AUTHOR

We buy what we are and we are what we buy.

Michael "wrote the book" on understanding consumers. Literally. Hundreds of thousands of business students have learned about Marketing from his books including *Consumer Behavior: Buying, Having, and Being* -- the most widely used book on the subject in the world.

Much in demand as a keynote speaker, Michael often is asked to provide briefings to global executive teams who want significant increases in their bottom line and who understand that's accomplished by a deeper connection with their customers.

Michael's mantra: *We don't buy products because of what they do. We buy them because of what they mean.* He advises global clients in leading industries such as apparel and footwear (Calvin Klein, Levi Strauss, Under Armour, Timberland), financial services and e-commerce (eBay, Progressive), CPG (Procter & Gamble, Campbell's), retailing (H&M), sports (CrossFit, Philadelphia Eagles), manufacturing (DuPont, PP&G) and transportation (BMW, United Airlines) on marketing strategies to make them more consumer-centric. He regularly appears on television shows including *The Today Show*, *Good Morning America* and *CNN* to comment on consumer issues, and he is frequently quoted in major media outlets such as *The New York Times, USA Today, Adweek* and *Time*.

Michael received his Ph.D. in Social Psychology at The University of North Carolina at Chapel Hill. He has been a full-time faculty member at New York University, Rutgers University, and Auburn University and a part-time professor at The University of Manchester (U.K.), the Technical University of Lisbon (Portugal) and IESEG (France). He is currently Professor of Marketing (in the Haub School of Business at Saint Joseph's University in Philadelphia).

As an industry consultant, Michael combines cutting-edge academic theory with actionable real-world strategies. He helps managers get inside the heads of their customers so they can anticipate and satisfy their deepest and most pressing needs – today and tomorrow. An executive at Subaru said it best: "The man is a scholar who is current and street-wise."

OTHER BOOKS BY MICHAEL SOLOMON

Consumer Behavior: Buying, Having and Being 12th edition
Marketing: Real People, Real Choices 9th edition
Social Media Marketing 3rd edition
The Routledge Companion to Consumer Behavior
The Truth About What Customers Want
Conquering Consumerspace: Marketing Strategies for a Branded World
Virtual Social Identity and Consumer Behavior
Consumer Behavior: In Fashion, 2nd edition
Consumer Behaviour: A European Perspective, 6th edition
Launch: Advertising and Promotion in Real Time
The Psychology of Fashion

To learn about my other books please go here:
www.michaelsolomon.com

THINK OUT OF THE BOX.
Your Customers Are!

There are Two Kinds of People....
People who think there are two kinds of
people, and people who don't.

Why is our urge to think in absolutes so pervasive? One simple answer: This is the way our brains work. Psychologists know that when we encounter a new object (or person), within milliseconds our immediate response is to put it into a familiar category. Good or bad? Weak or strong? Binary code: 0 or 1? Regular or decaf? Ready-to-wear or *haute couture*? Swipe left or swipe right?

Build a wall, and firmly plant people on one side or the other. Perhaps this mindset is a holdover from the caveman days, when the choice about how to label a person literally was life-or-death. Imagine a prehistoric man wandering across the savannah. Suddenly he spies a stranger heading his way. It's time for a really quick judgment call: Friend or foe? The wrong answer can turn out quite badly for him, to say the least. Today we short-circuit this dilemma with a handshake, a gesture that evolved to assure others that you are not holding a weapon. Even with this more civilized solution, our "good-or-bad" decision process isn't that much different from our ancient forefathers.

This book is about putting consumers into neat little categories -- and why unlike that comforting handshake this familiar habit can come back to bite you. You may find it convenient, but your customers sure don't. They want to be liberated. But don't despair -- that yearning to escape from walls also opens opportunities for you. Let's see how.

A Chinese curse decrees, "May you live in interesting times."

These certainly are interesting times for marketers. For years, we've put customers into tidy little boxes, such as age groups, income groups or gender groups. Business school professors (*mea culpa*) indoctrinate the next generation of executives to this way of thinking: We teach our MBA students about tidy 2 x 2 experimental designs that vary some factors and hold others constant so that we can identify what causes changes in consumer behavior. If we do observe a change after we manipulate one or more variables, we are more confident that something in what we varied caused the shift. Even then, we're never certain – most studies establish a confidence level of $p < .05$, which means that the odds are less than 5% that the change we witness was caused by chance. After all, the most rigorous study cannot <u>totally</u> establish a causal link. The best we can do is to increase our confidence in the likelihood that altering one variable causes a change in another. Scientists who make a more definitive statement than that are operating above their pay grade.

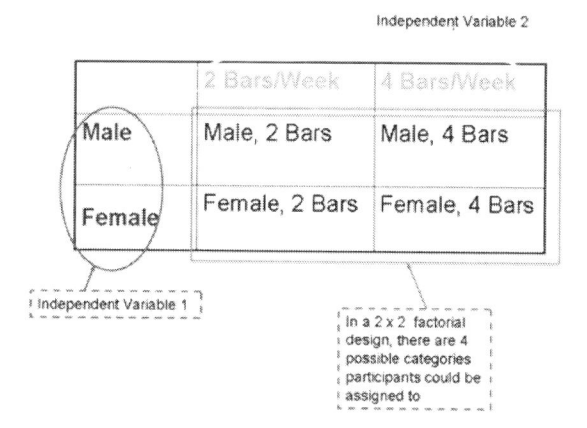

A typical 2x2 experimental design.

In another Marketing lecture to our MBAs, we extol the value of the widely used *BCG growth-share matrix*. This allows the strategist to classify a firm's product portfolio in terms of a category's growth rate and a brand's relative growth rate. Again, we construct a comforting 2 x 2 scheme that allows us to distinguish among cash cows, dogs, stars, and question marks.

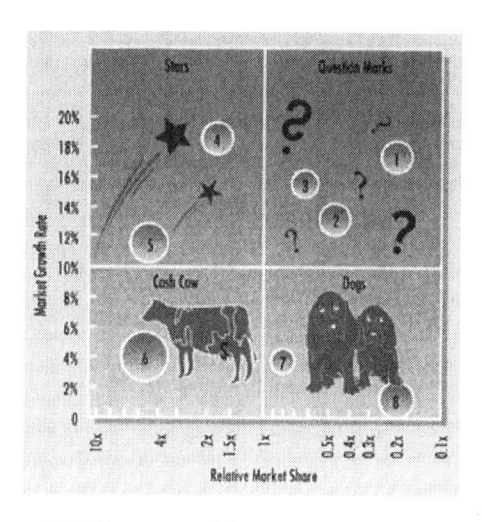

The widely used BCG (courtesy of the Boston Consulting Group) growth-share matrix puts a firm's product portfolio into tidy little boxes.

At least since General Motors pioneered the concept of *market segmentation* in the 1940s (Chevrolets for some, Cadillacs for others), we've assigned labels to consumers. Then we develop products and services for those who land in each neat box. Marketing strategy is largely about dichotomies: Male or female. Introvert or extravert. Light user or heavy user. Black or white. No room for shades of gray (much less 50 shades!).

Market segmentation: Cadillac for some, Chevy for others.

The Truth is Out There

Why are these walls everywhere we look in marketing? Like their counterparts in the hard sciences, most social scientists (including this one) cut their teeth on the hallowed *scientific method*. This paradigm relies upon strict categorization and an objective, unbiased perspective to understand what's going on in the world. The *modernism* philosophy that gave birth to this approach rebelled against many centuries of a culture dominated by what its founders viewed as baseless superstitions and religious hypocrisies. In its place, the new "religion" of the late 19th and early 20th centuries worshipped technology and practical experimentation. Function took precedence over form. The Industrial Revolution elevated engineering over art.

The clean lines of a skyscraper illustrate the modernist approach to design.

The *modernist*, or *positivist*, searches for objective facts. Through a process of systematic discovery, he or she believes it is possible to identify basic laws that govern the way things work in this world. The truth is out there. We just have to find it.

A basic dichotomy scientists revere is *In Here vs. Out There*. To study a phenomenon we need to isolate it from its naturally occurring context. This enables us to eliminate "confounds" that may obscure the true cause of what we observe. We dutifully take a sample, bring it into a sterile laboratory, and manipulate it while we hold everything else constant. If we observe any changes after we're done, we have much greater confidence that they relate to what we did, rather than to some other unruly stuff going on in the real world. "Just the facts, ma'am."

Unfortunately this positivist approach doesn't always work so well in the social sciences, where we study messy people who don't necessarily behave the same way in a lab as they do in the real world. Although many marketing researchers still pursue "the truth" via laboratory research, we're also witnessing a rebirth of qualitative methods like *ethnography* that encourage analysts to observe their customers in their natural settings.

Welcome to the wild, wacky world of the *postmodern consumer*. To truly understand today's customer, it's often smart to use *naturalistic techniques* that require researchers to "live with the natives." In other words, observe how consumers actually use products in their everyday habitats. Fish where the fish are.

> ## GRAB YOUR SLEDGEHAMMER
> Breach the wall that separates you from your customers. Get out of your office and meet the people who love your brand. Don't forget to talk to some who don't as well. Fish where the fish are.

But let the seller beware: Things get messier in the real world where our customers actually live – and buy. Sure, we reap a lot of rich insights. But because there's a lot of "stuff" going on out there (some call it "life") be sure to apply a grain of salt when you interpret the results. Controlled laboratory studies are much more sterile – but unfortunately in more ways than one. Although we may pick up a lot of static in natural environments, we also get a level of richness that is very hard to come by in more formal research settings. Cast your net wide, and don't be surprised if not all of what you catch is usable. However, the fish that remain will be well worth the trip.

Apples to Apples

Another reason we love to put things in categories is simple efficiency. When we place an object in a tidy group, we have something to compare it to. The product joins other brands we have assigned to that category as well. An industry develops specifications and nomenclature to apply across brands within a vertical. A retailer knows where to display an item in the store. Shoppers know where to find that item.

If we can compare apples to apples, it's easy to see how a brand stacks up against competitors. We can decide if a brand is "best in class" -- a good or bad representative of that category -- by comparing it to other members.

An apple and a tomato both belong in the "fruit" category, but you can guess which is a better exemplar.

A consumer doesn't evaluate a refrigerator in isolation; she compares its attributes to those of other refrigerators she has already considered. Similarly, a brand manager doesn't promote a product in isolation; she identifies immediate competitors and positions her brand (ideally) to emphasize areas where she excels and downplay those where she doesn't. Those qualities on which the brand excels are its *determinant attributes*. That's why marketers devote a lot of effort (or at least they should) to answering the basic strategic question, "What market am I in?"

The answer often isn't as obvious as you'd like to believe. To invoke one of the most tried-and-true marketing stories, the Railroad Barons of the late 19th century who ultimately succeeded were those who figured out that contrary to popular belief they were not in the railroad business. When they redefined their industry more broadly as transportation, they were able to compete against the newfangled automobiles and trucks that appeared on the scene. Those who weren't agile enough to make the switch suffered from a classic case of *marketing myopia* – and they paid the consequences.[1]

GRAB YOUR SLEDGEHAMMER

Don't get hemmed in by a wall of your own making. What business are you in – really? Answer this seemingly obvious question not in terms of what you produce, but what people consume. If you run a dance company, your competitors include other dance companies – but also perhaps museums, cooking classes, or even bars. Remember, a company makes pillows, but buyers consume sleep.

Apples, Oranges ... and Throw in Some Strawberries: Market Disruptions Destroy Categories!

Market disruptions happen when a brand refuses to play by the category rules. Netflix destroyed the video rental business. Uber threatens to do the same to the taxi industry. Books that are available in online form (perhaps like the one you're reading now) redefine how we acquire knowledge.

Sometimes this insubordination works against a product: A high-end dog food that had to be sold in the grocery's refrigerated section failed, because shoppers just didn't think of finding pet supplies there. An epilator for men failed for a different reason: Males couldn't swallow the idea of hair removal that didn't involve the testosterone-laden act of shaving. The new solution was more efficient. It just didn't fit conveniently into the customer's expectations about male versus female products.

But wait – under the right circumstances going against the grain actually creates wonderful opportunities. What if a marketer creates a new category, possibly by merging two existing ones? Chrysler fused a station wagon with a sedan to invent the minivan. This new category then spawned yet another, with the advent of the modern SUV in the 1990s. *Wearable technology* fuses fashion accessories with computers, so a stylish woman can wear a piece of Swarovski jewelry that also happens to monitor her heart rate.

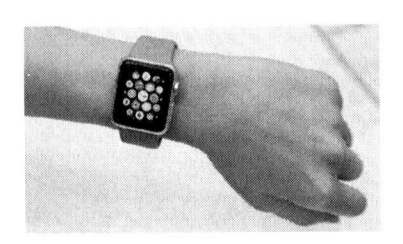

Is it tech? Is it jewelry? Why not both?

Today, we see a great example of this fusion strategy in the apparel business. The industry is showing anemic growth with one exception:

Athleisure. This stepchild of leisure clothing and athletic clothing (formerly two distinct categories) has created an entirely new market, and a cultural phenomenon as well. The term athleisure recently entered the *Merriam-Webster Dictionary*. And, Morgan Stanley projects global sales of this new entity will exceed $350 billion by 2020.[2]

The yoga craze fuels the athleisure phenomenon.

Now comes the "interesting" part of that Chinese curse: As we see in the case of the athleisure hybrid, today's consumers no longer yearn for conventional categories. They're climbing out over the walls we put them in. Like leisurewear versus athletic wear, the basic assumptions we use to make sense of the market have collapsed.

What's also "interesting" is that these dichotomies are embedded so deeply that managers don't even think about them – until they disappear. Fundamental categories that form the bedrock of marketing strategy and customer insights no longer exist. It's a management cliché to exhort employees to "think outside the box," but when it comes to customer insights perhaps we need to take this expression a bit more literally. Don't just think outside the box – throw the whole box away.

GRAB YOUR SLEDGEHAMMER

Carefully identify the categories your industry uses to define offerings. Then demolish them. Maybe you can fuse a fashion product with a functional one. For example, some pioneers in the emerging "smart garment" domain look at a pair of panty hose, but they see something other than silky legs: A "delivery system" that can literally apply vitamins, medications and caffeine (that reduces the appearance of cellulite) to the body. Just add some microencapsulation to the fibers, and you're playing in a whole new space.

Hybrid products and services that combine features of two or more existing verticals get to define the rules for a brand new category – at least until someone else tears down that wall as well.

The Omnichannel Consumer

We hear a lot of buzz today about *omnichannel marketing*. It's pretty much a foregone conclusion that organizations need to expand their thinking beyond which channel they will use to reach their customers. Instead, they need to ask which channels they need to be on, whether TV, social media, print, etc.

But we also need to think about the *omnichannel consumer*. Today's customer thinks in several modalities at once, and s/he transforms into different types of people many times in a day. Just who is the consumer at the other end of these channels?

The fluidity of *consumer identity* actually is not a new story. A chapter in Douglas Coupland's influential 1991 book *Generation X* declared, "I am not a market segment."[3] People have been trying on different personalities for years as they strive to break out of their own little boxes. We've come a long way from the drab, conforming "Organization Man" of the 1950s.

A consumer's consumption choices are a lot more varied and complicated than they used to be, as seemingly endless options to spend our time and money entice us.

Still, until recently the splintering of lifestyle groups was fairly restrained. Flower children in the 1960s did their own thing, but because most were tuned in to the big record labels and magazines of the time everyone's sartorial rebellion looked pretty much the same. Are those your tie-dyed jeans or mine?

The "do your own thing" revolution in the 1960's ironically morphed into just another popular style.

Fast forward to today, when we truly live in an era of *market fragmentation*. Just as our TV viewing options have expanded from three major networks in the 1960s to thousands of channels today, the monolithic market segments of that time have decomposed into innumerable *micro-segments*. The postmodern consumer blithely travels from one to another. The only constant we can count on is that s/he will change, and probably quickly.

To see this splintering in action, just visit any decent-sized magazine stand. Count the staggering number of publications that give us a glimpse into obscure lifestyles ranging from yachting to coding to pumping iron. Stroll through the food court in a typical shopping mall. You can choose from a dizzying range of ethnic foods – Chinese, Italian, American, sushi, Thai, and Mexican -- perhaps all on the same plate.

The food court in a shopping mall is a shrine to postmodernism.

Clearly the "one size fits all" (or at least "three networks fit all") model has to go. At least a handful of consumer behavior researchers have advocated a more fluid approach to understanding our brand choices for quite awhile. These *interpretivists* like to muddy the waters rather than clearing them up. They stress the importance of symbolic, subjective experience, and the idea that meaning is in the mind of the person. In this view, we each construct our own beliefs based upon our unique and shared cultural experiences, so there are no objectively right or wrong answers. No black and white, just shades of gray. "Beauty is in the eye of the beholder." "One man's meat is another man's poison." "That's why they make chocolate and vanilla." You get the idea…

In this *postmodern* view, our world is a *pastiche*, or mixture of images and ideas.[4] Our consumption choices are most valuable when they question boundaries and force us to venture outside of our little boxes. We see the impact of postmodernism most vividly when we look at how consumers around the world integrate foreign products with indigenous practices in a process of *creolization*:

- The Indian music hybrid called *Indipop* mixes traditional styles with rock, rap, and reggae.[5]

- Natives in Papua New Guinea pound on drums adorned with Chivas Regal wrappers and substitute Pentel pens for their traditional nose bones.[6]

- Young Hispanic Americans bounce between hip-hop and *Rock en Español*, blend Mexican rice with spaghetti sauce, and spread peanut butter and jelly on tortillas.[7]

- In Turkey some urban women use their ovens to dry clothes and rinse muddy spinach in their dishwashers.

- When an Ethiopian princess marries a Zulu king, tribesmen watch "Pluto Tries to Become a Circus Dog" on a Viewmaster while a band plays "The Sound of Music."[8]

In today's "interesting times," technological and societal changes free up more of us to be cultural chameleons. The fragmentation of society, and of media, exposes the consumer to many more *possible selves*. A *postmodern society* that refutes the tenets of *modernism* by blending categories together allows us to experiment with new options. It demolishes the walls.

Between 1975 and 2008, the number of products in the average supermarket swelled from an average of 8,948 to almost 47,000, according to the Food Marketing Institute.

The postmodern consumer actually is many consumers. We change our identities faster than a chameleon changes color. On Monday, you may be a Hugo Boss suit-wearing salaryman who listens to Adele, reads *The Wall Street Journal*, quaffs a greasy burger for lunch, and tunes in to *Fox News*. Come Saturday, the tats emerge from underneath the starched collar, you ditch the suit for a Kid Dangerous tee and Vans kicks, you down a tuna poké with a craft beer, and listen to Imagine Dragons while you check out the latest issue of *High Times*. Just what lifestyle category do you belong to?

Today's consumer changes colors faster than a chameleon.

The postmodern revolution requires marketers to revisit the walls they've erected over many years. That's not an easy thing to do. Conventional marketing strategies are built upon predictability, stability and the comfort in knowing that we can "understand" our customer yesterday, today and tomorrow. To accomplish this we love to put people into categories and often into super-neat dichotomies – and call it a day.

In this book, we'll visit seven of these basic categories (and lots of others too). Then we'll show why they no longer exist. Their collapse signals earthshaking changes for marketing and consumer behavior going forward. These shifts in the basic bedrock of the marketing landscape in turn require us to rethink what we think we know about consumers -- and the way they think about marketers.

WALL #1:
Us vs. Them

Let's start with some of the "easy" categories we commonly use to segment markets. *Demographics* are statistics that measure observable aspects of a population, including age, gender, ethnic group, income, etc. These broad categories typically are the "go-tos" when any marketer wants to subdivide a mass audience. It's Wall Building 101.

In a stable, relatively homogeneous society this strategy makes a lot of sense. It certainly did for General Motors in the early part of last century. Henry Ford famously boasted that his customers could have any color Model T they wanted – as long as it was black. Alfred Sloane and his colleagues at GM thought differently. They had the insight that drivers at various income levels would be prime customers for autos that sold at a range of price points. They created the Oldsmobile, Chevrolet, Cadillac, Pontiac and Buick divisions, and market segmentation was on its way.

Demographic segmentation requires the marketer to identify reasonably large segments of people s/he can reliably place into an observable category. Uh oh. That's not as easy as it used to be. A society in flux constantly redefines these basic categories, to the point where we must challenge even our fundamental assumptions about the convenient little boxes that organizations like the U.S. Census Bureau want to place us in. Let's revisit some of the most important – and perhaps obsolete – demographic dichotomies:

Young Vs. Old

"Sixty is the new forty!" "You're only as old as you feel." "Youth is wasted on the young." It's no secret that we live in a youth-oriented society – but also one that is reinventing the concept of ageing. Marketers rely heavily on the idea of *age cohorts* as they devise new products and messaging campaigns. They love to toss around categories like Gen X, Gen Y and now Gen Z. But when elementary school age girls (and younger!) wear jewelry and high heels on TV beauty pageants like *Toddlers and Tiaras* while octogenarians run marathons (there were 15 of them in the 2015 Boston Marathon), maybe these convenient categories don't work so well anymore.

It's true that the era in which you grow up bonds you with the millions of others who came of age during the same time period. Obviously, your needs and preferences evolve as you grow older—often in concert with others of your own age. For this reason, our age is a big part of our identity. All things equal, we are more likely to have things in common with people our own age than with those younger or older. These similarities can create opportunities for marketers, or they can raise red flags: Younger consumers, for example, don't drink nearly as much coffee on a daily basis as do older people so the coffee industry needs to worry a bit.[9]

Still, to a large extent age categories are a *social construction* – they exist primarily in the eye of the beholder. Research confirms the popular wisdom that age is more a state of mind than of body. A person's mental outlook and activity level have a lot more to do with longevity and quality of life than his or her chronological age." That's why *perceived age*, or how old a person feels, is a better yardstick to use. Researchers measure perceived age on several dimensions, including "feel-age" (i.e., how old a person feels) and "look-age" (i.e., how old a person looks).[10] The older consumers get, the younger they feel relative to their actual age.

On the younger end of the spectrum, it's instructive to remember that the hallowed idea of being a "teenager" is a very new one. Another social construction. Throughout most of history, this stage of life simply didn't exist. There were no Gidgets in ancient Greece, or for that matter in our colonial past. Children reached a certain age (usually around puberty), perhaps underwent a rite-of-passage ritual (maybe venturing into the jungle alone to kill a wild beast and bring it home), and then without further ado were inducted into the adult workforce. Keep in mind that the "star-crossed lovers" Romeo and Juliet were 15 and 13, respectively.

The Gidget of the 1950s represented a new social construction: The teenager.

The magazine *Seventeen* helped to pioneer the concept of a transitional period for young people. When it first published in 1944, its founders realized that modern young women didn't want to be little clones of Mom. Following World War II, the teenage conflict between rebellion and conformity began to unfold as an emerging youth culture pitted Elvis Presley, with his slicked hair and suggestive pelvis swivels, against the wholesome Pat Boone, with his white bucks and whiter teeth.

But it wasn't until 1956 when the label *teenager* entered the general American vocabulary. Frankie Lymon and the Teenagers became the first pop group to identify themselves with this new subculture. Today, this rebellion continues to play out as pubescent consumers forsake their Barbie dolls for the likes of Paris Hilton, Lindsay Lohan (when they're not in jail or rehab), Justin Bieber, or the teen heartthrob *du jour*.[11]

Kids vs. Teens

Even within the youth market the dichotomy between children and teenagers no longer holds water. Marketers refer to kids aged 8 to 14 as *tweens*, because they are "between" childhood and adolescence, and they exhibit characteristics of both age groups. Many marketers want to appeal to these consumers – they spend about $43 billion annually! Tweens are keen to experiment with products that make them appear older, even though they may not be psychologically or physically ready.

Abercrombie & Fitch crossed the line way back in 2002, when the clothing chain had to pull a line of thong underwear for young girls after many parents protested. Since that time, however, the line between childhood and adolescence continues to blur. In 2005, the NPD Group reported that the average age at which women began to use beauty products was 17. By 2009, that average had dropped to 13. Another study by Experian found that 43 percent of 6- to 9-year-olds use lipstick or lip-gloss, and 38 percent use hairstyling products.

GRAB YOUR SLEDGEHAMMER

A previous generation warned, "Never trust anyone over 30." That's definitely not the case today. Many Millennials are very tight with their parents. The majority of them think of Mom and Dad as friends. More incredibly, over half of view them as their best friends. A classic study conducted in 1972 identified what the authors termed the "Romeo and Juliet Effect" to describe the finding that increases in parental interference made it more likely that kids would persevere in a romantic relationship. A replication attempt in 2014 failed.

Parents are no longer the enemy. Anecdotally, I've heard from several retailers that mother-daughter shopping expeditions are very common (not to mention the joint credit card usage I observe in my own family – welcome to my life!). Marketers and merchants can do much more to celebrate this new buying duo. Incentivize parent/child activity and remember that it's no longer about looking as different from one another as possible. Today, it could be that what's good for the goose is also good for the gosling. Is the traditional wall that separates Parent vs. Friend eroding as well?

Old vs. Mature

The *Baby Boomer* age subculture consists of people whose parents established families following the end of World War II and during the 1950s when the peacetime economy was strong and stable. Boomers aren't exactly hanging out in rocking chairs quite yet – in fact they are six percent more likely than the national average to engage in some kind of sports activity.[12] And even demographers who love to put people into age categories distinguish between two subgroups of Baby Boomers: *Leading-edge boomers*, born between 1946 and 1955, grew up during the Vietnam War and Civil Rights eras. *Trailing-edge boomers*, who were born between 1956 and 1964, came of age after Vietnam and the Watergate scandal.[13]

Many marketers seem to have decided that if you can remember watching Ed Sullivan on Sunday nights, you're in the "old" category and not worthy of their attention. That's a mistake. In fact, Boomers spend 38.5 percent of CPG (consumer packaged goods) dollars. However, Nielsen estimates that only five percent of advertising dollars are currently targeted toward adults 35 to 64 years old.

Nielsen's research says that Boomers dominate 1,023 out of 1,083 CPG categories, and watch 9.34 hours of video per day—more than any other segment. They also constitute a third of all TV viewers, online users, social media users, and Twitter users, and are significantly more likely to have broadband Internet. As a Nielsen executive observed:

> Marketers have this tendency to think the Baby Boom—getting closer to retirement—will just be calm and peaceful as they move ahead, and that's not true. Everything we see with our behavioral data says these people are going to be active consumers for much longer. They are going to be in better health, and despite the ugliness around the retirement stuff now, they are still going to be more affluent. They are going to be an important segment for a long time.[14]

This misconception is even more marked for Boomers' parents. Many marketers seem to picture a senior consumer as a recluse who is in poor health, and who only buys necessities when they go on sale. The newer, more accurate profile of a "Silver Surfer" is an active person who is interested in what life has to offer, who is an enthusiastic consumer with the means and willingness to buy many goods and services, and who maintains strong loyalty to favorite brands over the years.

Think about this: The United Nations says that people older than 60 are the fastest-growing age group on Earth. There are 700 million of them now, and there will be two billion by midcentury. In the United States, by the year 2030 20 percent of the population will be over the age of 65.[15] By 2100, there will be 5 million of us who are at least 100 years old.[16]

Few of us may be around then, but we can already see the effects of the *senior market* today. Older adults control more than 50 percent of discretionary income, and worldwide consumers over the age of 50 spend nearly $400 billion a year.[17] We're living longer and healthier lives because of more wholesome lifestyles (at least some of us), improved medical diagnoses and treatment, and changing cultural expectations about appropriate behaviors for the elderly. Larger numbers of older people lead more active, multidimensional lives than we assume. Nearly 60 percent engage in volunteer activities, one in four seniors aged 65 to 72 still works, and more than 14 million provide care for their grandchildren.[18]

It is also crucial to remember that income alone does not express seniors' spending power. Older consumers are finished with many of the financial obligations that siphon off the income of younger consumers. Eighty percent of consumers older than age 65 own their own homes. In addition, child-rearing costs are over. As the popular bumper sticker proudly proclaims, "We're Spending Our Children's Inheritance!" Some of the important areas that stand to benefit from the surging gray market include exercise facilities, cruises and tourism, cosmetic surgery and skin treatments, and "how-to" books and university courses that offer enhanced learning opportunities.

A study investigated what the authors call consumer identity renaissance; this refers to the redefinition process people undergo when they retire. The research identified two different types of identity renaissance: revived (revitalization of previous identities) or emergent (pursuit of entirely new life projects). Even though retirees often have to deal with loss (of professional identity, spouses, and so on), many of them focus on moving forward. They engage in a host of strategies to do this, including affiliation, where they reconnect with family members and friends (in many cases online), and self-expression. This latter strategy may involve revisiting an activity they never had time to adequately pursue when they were younger, learning new skills, or perhaps moving into an urban area to reengage with cultural activities.[19] Marketers in turn stand to benefit from all of this activity if they stop sticking seniors behind that stubborn wall.

GRAB YOUR SLEDGEHAMMER

Age is a social construction. Try to talk to consumers, especially relatively older ones, in terms of perceived age rather than chronological age.

And, while it's tempting to pursue the young, hip and trendy (or whatever they call that these days), don't ignore the potential of "older" customers (even those over 40!).

Black vs. White

Until fairly recently, in a business sense many marketers thought in terms of a very simple racial dichotomy: White vs. Not Interested. If ethnic minorities appeared in a TV show or commercial, they played subservient or comical roles like the Aunt Jemima "Mammy" character. Advertisers focused exclusively on their (white) bread-and-butter– the so-called "general market" (code for white consumers) that held the purse strings in the U.S.A.

It took some simple financial data to wake up much of the business world to the overlooked economic clout of non-Caucasian consumers. The combined buying power of African-Americans, Asians and Native Americans was $1.4 trillion in 2007, a gain of 201 percent since 1990. Meanwhile, the economic clout of Latinos rose by 307 percent, to $862 billion, over that span.[20]

Predictably, as the word got out advertising agencies began to fall all over themselves to develop or acquire multicultural specialists who could talk to nonwhite consumers. Soon we were blanketed with targeted ads, shows and products that spoke exclusively to African Americans or Hispanics. The "Not Interested" segment splintered into very specific ethnic and racial groups, each with its own unique subcultural advertising references and images calculated to heighten identification with mainstream brands. Suddenly there were a lot of categories to contend with. Each segment was put it into its own tidy little silo and pursued by specialized agencies.

Finally these overlooked markets got the attention they deserved. But ironically, it looks like many American consumers – even minorities who were ignored or dissed before – are growing weary of the silos in which the marketing industry has placed them. They are starting to crave more of the "melting pot" vision of America than a neatly compartmentalized world where each group gets its own separate (even if equal) attention. A recent study that surveyed over 2,000 people reported that 80 percent of parents like to see diverse families in advertisements. Sixty-six percent said that brands that showed reverence for all kinds of families was an important factor when they chose among competing options.[21]

The U.S.A. is coalescing as a multicultural society, despite the political rhetoric about the impact of immigrants on our economy. We're far from out of the woods, obviously, but there's cause for optimism. When Cheerios ran a controversial commercial featuring a biracial family in 2013, the company had to shut down the comments section on its YouTube channel due to racist posts. General Mills ran a sequel featuring the same family in the 2014 Super Bowl, and the ad was a huge success with over 5 million YouTube views recorded.[22]

The rapidly growing diversity of American culture is one of the most important drivers of change in this century. The U.S. Census Bureau projects that by 2018 it won't be possible to place a majority of children under the age of 18 into a single racial or ethnic group. That helps to explain why about 6% of people who filled out the last Census didn't select one of the race categories the form provided.[23]

> ## GRAB YOUR SLEDGEHAMMER
> The walls that separate ethnic and racial subcultures continue to come down, as Americans increasingly regard themselves as members of multiple groups. The millennial generation is the most diverse our country has ever seen. Consumers increasingly take for granted that products and advertising will blend these identities rather than cater only to a specific subculture. Don't be afraid to blend subcultures in your messages.

The Census Bureau also predicts that by 2050, people who identify themselves as multiracial will make up almost four percent of the U.S. population. Among American children, the multiracial population has increased almost 50 percent, to 4.2 million, since 2000, making it the fastest growing youth group in the country. The number of people of all ages who identified themselves as both white and black soared by 134 percent since 2000 to 1.8 million people.[24] As you can see, people aren't just thinking outside the box. They're jumping out of it!

WALL #2:
Me vs. We

1967: Mary joyfully hangs up the kitchen phone: Skip has finally asked her to the Senior Prom! She immediately dials her best friend Jane to share the news. Jane excitedly tells Mary about the gorgeous dress she saw in the window of Bon Ton Fashions downtown that would be perfect for the event. Jane borrows her Dad's Dodge Dart, and they round up two more friends and drive to the store. Mary tries on the dress, along with six other alternatives as her friends critique each. After two hours of parading in and out of the dressing room to show off each option, the group delivers its verdict: that first one was The Dress all along. Mary counts out the $50 in carefully folded bills she's been saving from her allowance and drives home with her prize. Six weeks later she picks up her Prom photos and she mails a set to each of her proud grandparents and other family members.

2017: Madison, Mary's daughter, sits in her History class idly scrolling through some of her favorite fashion blogs; just a typical Wednesday in high school. It's May, and so many of her clothing gurus are chatting about the latest trends in prom styles. On a whim, Madison texts Silas to see if he and his bros are going to the Senior Prom. Silas replies yes, and he asks her to come to the dance with them as well as to the overnight after-party. Madison immediately posts gossip about who will be at the uber-cool after-party on Facebook, and she texts Mary with the news. As she sits in Algebra class later that day, she Googles '"senior prom wear." She starts to pin dresses to several of her Pinterest Boards, which she shares with her Facebook friends. An hour later, Madison receives a Pinterest "Fashion Boards Outfits" notification on her iPhone. She reads what others have posted about the outfits; many seem to like the one she pinned from Bon Ton. As she sits in her Prius before driving home from school, Madison visits the Bon Ton website. She creates her personal virtual model to try on some dresses.

When Madison shares screenshots with her friends online, she's disappointed to see that most of them give the highest number of stars to one dress that's a bit out of her price range. On a hunch she goes on her Gilt app, and sure enough that exact dress is 60% off! Of course, there's a catch: there are only 25 in stock, and then the offer is over. Her heart pounds as she sees on the real-time message board that 15 dresses have been sold in the last hour. Madison jumps on the deal - she pays with her Mom's PayPal account and figures Mary will be fine with that since she found such a bargain.

Two days later, UPS delivers the dress and sure enough it fits like a glove (literally). On Prom Night, Madison takes a selfie, posts it to Instagram and shares it on Facebook, Twitter and Tumblr, where she receives many Likes and comments. The next day, Madison links the previous comments to her photos, and she recommends the brand. She also writes a positive review on the brand's Facebook page. Lastly, she browses the brand's website and creates additional looks, which she uploads to Pinterest to ease the way for others who will face the same dilemma. Hooking up with Silas was okay, but the important thing is that she snagged a great deal and earned the respect of her *fashionista* network. And, her mother Mary will be thrilled to see her looking so grown up - if she can finally teach Mom how to log on to her Facebook page.[25]

Proms are as popular today as they were 50 years ago, but the experience has changed with the times.

The Old School, Linear Model of Consumer Decision Making

Mary's 1967 Prom story conforms to over 50 years of consumer behavior research that shows people engage in a systematic, linear sequence as they process information prior to purchase. But her daughter's 2017 experience shreds this fundamental assumption. Young shoppers like Madison force us to tear up much of what we know about how people decide what to buy. The tidy little boxes of decision-making activity are disintegrating before our eyes.

Rather than a predictable slow march toward a purchase decision, today we witness a steady stream of interactions with marketers including these:

- *Native marketing executions* that blur the lines between editorial and commercial messages

- Applications linked to the "Internet of Things" that enable companies to monitor our physical and mental well-being (and automatically restock us with medicine and food as necessary)

- Encounters with digital avatars and holographs

- Smartphone alerts that let us know a price we're watching has dropped

And many more. This constant barrage of information creates an *always-on shopper* who no longer distinguishes between consuming and non-consuming states of being. Consumers are open for business 24/7.

But let's take a step back. Just what do we (think) we know about how consumers decide what to buy? Our saga begins in 1968, when three academic researchers formalized and published a decision-making model that has guided a lot of explorations into how people choose one brand over others.[26] The model proposes a sequential process of decision making that consists of five separate stages:

1. Problem recognition
2. Information search
3. Evaluation of alternatives
4. Purchase
5. Post-purchase evaluation

This process typically starts with a consumer's conscious recognition of an unsatisfied need, whether for a new dress, a carton of milk, or a college education. It's grounded in the idea of a solitary, rational decision-maker who systematically accesses and sifts through information to maximize utility (that's economist-speak for "arrive at the best possible choice").

Thus Mary's decision-making process gets triggered when she's asked to the Prom. This invitation prompts her to recognize an unmet need – a dress for the event. Her response is to enlist her friends to help her to identify dress options and then to hone in on the one garment that will do the trick. Mary makes her choice, pays for the item and dances in style. Eventually she receives admiring feedback about her selection when she distributes photos from the big night to friends and family. The event triggers a need, she acquires and evaluates the information she needs to make a smart choice, and the approval she receives affirms the wisdom of her decision. End of story.

Today's Nonlinear Consumer Decision Making: Who Moved My ZMOT?

Fast forward to today, and we have a very different story. Madison's decision-making odyssey looks quite different from her mother's. It doesn't follow a predictable, comfortably linear path from problem recognition to purchase and post-purchase evaluation. Instead, the teenager's purchase decision seems to emerge almost randomly from a 24/7 barrage of inputs her social network provides, combined with her outputs in the form of ongoing Web and social media platform queries. Although Madison still experiences all the traditional stages of decision making, the process is no longer so neat and tidy. In fact it looks more like an organic, constant mutation than a series of steps we can isolate in real time.

GRAB YOUR SLEDGEHAMMER

Today's consumer no longer makes most decisions in a systematic, linear way. You need to stay in touch on a more constant basis – without being intrusive (easier said than done).

Your digital assets need to be "always on" so that the shopper who hits your app or website can access up-to-the minute info at will. Many younger consumers have much shorter attention spans, and we've taught them to expect instant gratification. You may not get a second chance, so get it right the first time.

ZMOT and Why it Matters

The wizards at Google talk a lot about something they label *ZMOT*. Here's how they define it:

> It's a new decision-making moment that takes place a hundred million times a day on mobile phones, laptops and wired devices of all kinds. It's a moment where marketing happens, where information happens, and where consumers make choices that affect the success and failure of nearly every brand in the world. At Google, we call this the Zero Moment of Truth, or simply ZMOT ("ZEE-mot").[27]

As it should be, Google is obsessed with ZMOT. After all, it's that magical moment when the consumer decides to buy. But because we've transformed into a highly mobile society, where and when ZMOT occurs has changed as well. Google and many other companies in the search business present tons of data to show that today ZMOT is just as, if not more, likely to occur at home, at work, in a car, or many places other than a store.

This profound change holds implications for other kinds of companies as well – in fact, for just about every organization out there. This is because these new ZMOTs upend the traditional linear decision-making model. Simply put, consumers not only have changed where they decide, but how as well.[28]

In particular, this transformation signals a move toward *buying by committee*. Contrary to the linear model's portrait of the decision maker as a lone wolf who only solicits feedback after the sale, the new "always-on" consumer constantly requests advice from her social network. She is far more likely to painstakingly research even the most minor purchases.

Ironically, the purchase dynamics of end consumers are starting to more closely resemble what we observe in industrial buying situations. In these contexts, members of a *buying center* (not a physical place!) play different roles as the team tackles a problem, evaluates its options and jointly decides on a solution. Some members are gatekeepers who control the flow of information, others actively research the available options, and still others render the final verdict. Today it seems that "it takes a village" to buy a prom dress, just as it does to choose a corporate computer system.

In the new age of *participatory consumption*, it's more true than ever that "no man is an island": A 2016 Pew Research Center survey found that 40% of Americans say they almost always consult online reviews before they buy something new.[29]

And, these individuals often assemble their own "buying center" that consists of friends (real ones), Facebook friends (i.e., digital ones they may never meet in person) and even automated recommendation agents who constantly troll the web searching for solutions if and when a problem surfaces.

The walls we have built over the years to partition the different stages of decision making just have to come down. Let's take a quick look at how the traditional stages of problem solving are changing even as you read this:

The (Traditional) Stages of Consumer Decision Making

1. Problem recognition

We're all too familiar with the eerie experience of people walking by us with their heads bent over their phones, oblivious to everything but what they view in their devices. Madison is immersed in her network, so she's constantly exposed to new "problems," i.e. needs and wants she didn't know she had until her network alerted her. Old-school advertising did the same to a limited extent, when marketers invented conditions like "halitosis" to make consumers uneasy about their breath. Still, those campaigns were infrequent, carefully planned, and expensive.

In contrast, today's consumers are constantly exposed to people's challenges and accomplishments that contribute to the ubiquitous state of anxiety that others are more popular, beautiful or accomplished. This condition even has a name: *FOMO (Fear of Missing Out)*. Many of us are always on high alert to meet the next social challenge as we troll the Internet to anticipate problems before they find us.

This vigilance takes its toll; several studies report that heavy usage of social media platforms like Facebook is related to feelings of unhappiness, loneliness and envy.[30] In a sense, problem recognition has morphed into an ongoing Google search as users ask, "How can I know what I want until I read what other people say?"

Things are looking...down.

2. Information search

Information search is big business. No kidding! In the U.S. alone, companies spend almost $40 billion per year on search advertising (Google pockets about 80% of that revenue).[31] But the real story isn't just how much we search. It's whom we ask.

In Mary's day, it was easy to identify the "fashion authorities" who decreed what was in and what was out in the pages of *Vogue* and the like. Madison may consult these anointed experts in passing, but she's far more likely to get the 411 on hot dress styles (and everything else) by checking out teenage fashion bloggers, Instagram photo feeds, and of course by asking her network. Today young *fashionistas* around the world who write blogs like *Creme De La Crop*, *Style Rookie*, and *Tolly Dolly Posh* rule the roost.[32]

And, Madison's search is increasingly more visual than text-based. The growth of image banks like Pinterest, coupled with image recognition technology, means that consumers can search for visual markers of a product rather than trying to describe it in words. For instance, *thehunt.com* takes a request for a garment or accessory; then it challenges community members to track it down. Just as the Shazam app (now owned by Apple) can tell you the name of a song that's playing right now on your radio, new software products from startups such as Snap Fashion, Style-Eyes and Slyce allow shoppers to take a picture of a garment on their smartphones and then link to a retailer where they can buy that piece or something similar.[33]

3. Evaluation of Alternatives

One of the most formidable challenges consumers face today is very much a "First World Problem:" We have far too many choices. While it's surely good to have options, at least in the developed world ironically we suffer from an abundance of riches. Want a new lipstick color? Here are 1000 or so. Need a lamp? Let's access the hundreds of styles in these online catalogs. This condition that researchers term *hyperchoice* unfortunately means that we have <u>too much of a good thing</u>. Numerous studies show that consumers actually make <mark>dumber decisions</mark> -- and <mark>feel more frustrated and angry</mark> – when they have a lot of choices than when they have relatively few.

The Internet enables us to turn on a fire hose of information whenever we request it. Now we urgently need the valves to manage this overwhelming flow of information, lest we get swept away. In other words, today we need <mark>help just to filter</mark> the vast river of <u>options</u> into a manageable choice set. <u>We have never needed editors more than we do today.</u>

Hence the growth of powerful new tools such as comparison matrices, filters, and ranking and scoring programs that allow us to customize our informational environment so that we only see a small fraction of the choices out there. The downside: Just as with the news, we tend only to "discover" what we already know and we don't learn about novel options. We are likely to inhabit what the Internet activist Eli Pariser famously calls a *filter bubble*.[34]

4. Purchase

In Mary's day, a bricks-and-mortar retailer (with a few exceptions such as TV sales, there was no other kind) competed with other physical stores for your business. In contrast, Madison may never set foot in a bricks-and-mortar structure to buy her dress. Eight in 10 Americans shop online today, over half have purchased something from their phones, and 15 percent bought something after they clicked through on a link shared on social media.[35] And, as chains like Best Buy have discovered, *showrooming* shoppers may come to regard the store as more of a convenient venue to test out a product before they buy it cheaper online.

Showrooming 101: Many shoppers treat the bricks-and-mortar store as an educational display area rather than as a place to buy.

This sea change illustrates a crucial point about the breakdown of the traditional linear decision-making model. Marketers typically view the magical moment when the consumer throws down her credit card as the final stop on the road to a purchase. Thus many selling strategies view the transaction as a way to seal the deal that has been forged previously via the steps of problem recognition, information search and evaluation of alternatives.

The purchase environment is the last chance to sway the customer, and increasingly marketers divert resources from traditional advertising and toward point-of-purchase messaging to make the sale in the store. This strategy still works well for small impulse purchases – who can pass up that alluring candy bar that's calling your name at the cash register?

But more and more retailers now confront shoppers who have already made up their minds before they park their cars in the lot. Over 80% of shoppers today conduct online research before they make a purchase, and 60% start the process by consulting an online search engine (the same percentage read product reviews before they buy).[36]

Thus Madison chose to search online bargain sites rather than purchase the dress she first encountered. Retailers no longer have the luxury of waiting to wow the customer when she walks in the door. They have to be part of the feedback loop much earlier than in the past. If they wait for the customer to stroll in before they turn on the selling charm, they will often be a "day late and a dollar short."

5. Post-Purchase Evaluation

Of course, savvy "relationship marketers" have known for a long time that the purchase usually isn't the end of the process at all. The real destination is post-purchase evaluation, which helps to determine whether the company has a shot to create a brand loyal customer down the road. They understand that it's far more expensive to acquire a new customer than to keep an old one, so you can't just rest on your laurels after the sale.

In the traditional model, the consumer receives feedback in the form of compliments (such as oohs and aahs from Mary's adoring grandparents when they get her Prom photos in the mail), an electric shock, a stomach ache, a clearer TV picture and so on, that validates or negates her choice. This *choice feedback* plays a key role in the learning process. Very simply, positive feedback makes it more likely the person will choose the same solution the next time the problem arises, while negative results steer him or her into the arms of a competitor. And, organizations that have figured this out will intermittently solicit their own feedback, in the form of surveys and other customer insights tools, to keep tabs on how they are doing post-sale.

In contrast, Madison lives in a world of constant feedback. She and her peeps spend each day posting virtually everything for evaluation by their social network. These posts include the infamous selfie, endless details about routine activities, even the meals she eats. Indeed the fascination with sharing glamorized photos of what's on our plates before we dig in has led to a craze popularly called *food porn*. It's gotten so out of control that some New York restaurants have banned the taking of selfies at their tables.[37]

> **GRAB YOUR SLEDGEHAMMER**
>
> It's far more expensive to acquire a new customer than to keep an old one. That's why you should think in terms of *lifetime customer value*, rather than in terms of discrete transactions. Follow up after the sale, and continue to vigorously court your customers. No matter how much they like you today, there are a lot of other potential suitors out there just waiting for you to drop the ball. *Customer relationship management* (CRM) databases and strategies that "mind the store" even when you don't are crucial to keep the ball rolling.

Here Comes Design Thinking

The battle for consumers' hearts, minds and wallets won't be won in R&D labs (sorry). Sure, shoppers love new gadgets and there's always room for innovation. However, the sad truth is that for the most part consumers don't see that much difference among competing brands – unless they're loyal followers of a *cult brand* like Apple, Nike or the Boston Red Sox.

And when they do form a strong preference for one particular offering, shoppers know that they have a multitude of ways to get it home. Some paths offer great convenience or even significant savings; others stimulate, educate or even titillate. A woman can order a pair of Vince Camuto ankle strap sandals online and wait for the friendly UPS man to pull up to her door two days later. Or, she can visit a bricks-and-mortar store where a friendly salesperson will fawn over her. While she's there, maybe she'll use an *augmented reality* "smart mirror" to see how the shoes will look with four different outfits. She may even take a selfie wearing the shoes, send it out to her "peeps" and get their reactions in real time before she takes the plunge. In all of these scenarios, the shoes get added to the collection that resides in her closet, but the experience of acquiring them is quite different.

It's that experience that is the value-added many retailers seek. An emphasis on the magic moment where the buyer interacts with the seller goes by many names: *Empathy. Customer-centric marketing. CX. The service encounter. Customer journeys.*[38]

No matter what you call it, a lot of companies are waking up to the urgent need to design with rather than design for their customers. It's no longer enough to phone it in by conducting a few focus groups in order to guess at what will resonate with buyers. The market moves too fast and product cycles have accelerated too dramatically to afford this luxury. Again, mass-market segmentation no longer makes much sense in a micro-targeted world.

A revolution in *design thinking* is afoot. The fundamental building blocks of this trending philosophy are EDIT: Empathize, Define, Ideate, and Test. You can't walk down this road without immersing yourself in your customer's perspective. So, empathy is the first big step. How can organizations truly understand the lived experiences of their customers so they can design new products and services that will resonate with them?

One offshoot of the design thinking revolution is the recognition that managers need to step out of their little boxes and actually cross over to the consumer's perspective to understand their products from the buyer's perspective. For this reason a big buzzword today is the *customer journey*.[39]

This methodology encourages brands to map out in excruciating detail all the steps a customer takes while they interact with the company – no matter where, and no matter how trivial. It's a powerful way to improve the experience. The journey spans a variety of *touchpoints* by which the customer moves from awareness to engagement and purchase. Successful brands focus on developing a seamless experience that ensures each touchpoint interconnects and contributes to the overall journey.

The consumer journey concept was influenced by the Japanese approach to *total quality management*. To help companies achieve more insight, researchers go to the *gemba*, which to the Japanese means "the one true source of information."[40] According to this philosophy, it's essential to send marketers and designers to the precise place where consumers use the product or service rather than to ask laboratory subjects to use it in a simulated environment. This approach syncs perfectly with the movement away from the sterile modernist research approaches we discussed earlier -- again, fish where the fish are. The postmodern consumer hates the laboratory.

A project by Host Foods illustrates this idea in practice. The company, which operates food concessions in major airports, sent a team to the *gemba*—in this case, an airport cafeteria—to identify problem areas. Employees watched as customers entered the facility, and then followed them as they inspected the menu, procured silverware, paid, and found a table.

The findings were crucial to Host's redesign of the facility. For example, the team identified a common problem that many people traveling solo experience: the need to put down one's luggage to enter the food line and the feeling of panic you get because you're not able to keep an eye on your valuables while you get your meal. This simple insight allowed Host to modify the design of its facilities to improve a patron's line-of-sight between the food area and the tables.[41]

A *customer journey map* is a tool that fits into the broader context of your customer experience strategy. It requires significant customer insight-driven inputs and internal buy-in to be effective. Maps aren't static -- customers and systems change over time – and they must be part of an effort that uses these insights to drive action, leading to actual improvements. Customer journey maps clarify what customers try to do, what barriers they face, and how they feel during each interaction with your product or service. Refining these smaller steps, such as how people complete a purchase online or file a complaint, is a primary way that journey maps improve the customer experience.[42] Again, these insights can only happen when managers climb over the wall that separates them from their customers.

The Rise of the Hive Mind

Back in the day, young people used to proudly proclaim, "Do your own thing." Today a more common refrain is, "What do my peeps think?" A constant immersion in social media creates a *hive mind*. It seems that before the consumer commits to a choice, decisions large and small – where to eat, what to wear, who to like – first need to be voted upon by his or her social network. That wall separating *Me vs. Them* is going, going, gone.

In many cases, the consumer makes a selection – but it doesn't "count" until he posts a photo to officially seal the deal. Anecdotally, many of my students have told me they didn't know the person they were dating broke up with them until they noticed s/he changed their relationship status on Facebook!

And then the process repeats again for the next choice – the hive hums 24/7. Indeed, a hard-core *Star Trek* fan is tempted to think of The Borg; an army of drones plugged into "The Collective" (or coincidentally "The Hive") that relentlessly assimilates technology from other species and absorbs them into its net. For marketers at least, The Borg's battle cry resonates: "Resistance is futile."

Today's "always on" consumer uses ubiquitous social media to access a hive mind.

The constant barrage of reactions to almost anything we say, buy, or do seems to propel us into a perpetual feedback loop. Our own satisfaction seems to largely be determined by what others in our *social graph* decree to be a good or bad choice.[43] Consumers seem to ask, "how can I know if I'm satisfied until I hear what <u>other</u> people say?"

Thousands of opinionated consumers have tapped into this *culture of commendation* by blogging and ==*vlogging* (video blogging)== to document their own purchase experiences in painstaking detail. These *haul videos* are so popular they have become their own genre on YouTube (along with *unpacking videos* that attract thousands of nerdy voyeurs who love to watch someone take a tech product out of a box and assemble it!).

"Haul videos" document a shopper's acquisitions in painstaking detail.

Indeed, these cinematic gems result in the accumulation of ==*online social capital*-- basically, "street cred"== from posting videos and enticing others to watch them -- that in time may even escalate into (minor) celebrity status. By cleverly promoting their online product evaluations, bloggers and vloggers can gain a large following and generate revenue from views and endorsements. If successful, they can create their own personal brands as they amass power and legitimacy in online marketplaces.

However such moments of fame are fleeting, as the Internet's span of attention grows ever shorter and our focus turns to the next *microcelebrity*. Many bloggers who aspire to be the next Perez Hilton or Kim Kardashian would be quite grateful for the "fifteen minutes of fame" Andy

Warhol promised each of us almost 50 years ago. Certainly former microstars such as Katy Perry's Left Shark in the 2017 Super Bowl show and "Alex from Target" would agree.

Katy Perry's "Left Shark" became a microstar – and then we're on to the next one.

Participatory Culture: Bowling Together

The *hive mind* is a large digital community of people who share their knowledge and opinions to keep members engaged in a constant feedback loop. This results in collective intelligence and concentric rings of group affinity that rely upon one another for validation of their choices.

This collective also highlights yet another wall that's come down: *Friend vs. Stranger*. The average Facebook user has 155 "friends," and many *aficionados* count 500+ people in their network.[44] When I poll my undergraduates on this question, typically at least ½ of them tell me they have at least 500 buddies. In the old days, a friend was someone you knew personally – and probably pretty well. Today we heed advice from "friends" in our social graph whom we have never met, and probably never will.

On auction sites like eBay, the knowledge that others are interested in acquiring that Elvis figurine or used Rolex heightens your own interest, and spurs bidders to offer amounts they might not consider spending in a traditional retail environment. Similarly, when Groupon shares how many others have purchased a deal in the last 24 hours this fosters an illusion of scarcity and also validates the urge to jump on the bandwagon.

In 2001, Robert Putnam's controversial book *Bowling Alone: The Collapse and Revival of American Community* chronicled the disintegration of traditional social institutions as people gravitated instead toward solitary pursuits such as surfing the Internet.[45] But a lot has changed since then. In the almost twenty years since this book was published, social media has reconnected us. At least in a digital sense, most of us are far from alone.

Indeed, today perhaps a more accurate metaphor to describe contemporary consumer behavior in the online world is no longer *bowling alone*, but *bowling by committee*. Consumers avidly post their opinions, experiences, and product reviews online and eagerly seek the posts of others in their social networks.[46] Before they enter a store, 62% of millennial shoppers already know what they want to buy from their research in the online environment, and 84% say that consumer-written content on brand websites influences what they buy.[47]

In stark contrast to the sequential paradigm of the old-school linear model, a hive mind is constantly buzzing -- and constantly acting. We've morphed into an endless state of *polysynchronous consumption*: A nonstop blending of multiple channels of asynchronous online and synchronous online communication that we access in tandem with our other activities via mobile phones and other devices.

We're back to bowling together – at least digitally.

The Hive Mind Makes Honey – and Money: Why Marketers Should Care

Madison's Prom shopping adventure shouldn't be shrugged off as just another example of the younger generation's limited attention span, or a sign that civilization as we know it will soon be over. Her constant movement between the borders that separate the online and offline worlds illustrates the challenges and opportunities that organizations face in an environment where the familiar, linear model of consumer decision making rapidly recedes in the rear-view mirror. The "always on" landscape upends many of our cherished assumptions about where, when and why customers engage with the marketplace.

Social Scoring

Why do people post so many photos that document silly pet costumes, a "selfie" at the dry cleaner, or the poké bowl they had for lunch? Because they can. The smartphone has turned each of us into a documentary filmmaker – and an *artiste* who is obsessed with how the "critics" will review the movie of his or her life. We've reached the point where reporting the activity seems to be more important than the activity itself. Researchers call this ongoing documentation *social scoring*.

In a typical day, people upload 350 million photos to Facebook. They share 1.3 million pieces of content on Facebook every minute of every day. On top of that, they send 500 million Tweets in a day, pin 14 million items on Pinterest, post 85 million videos and photos on Instagram, and still find time to view 25 million LinkedIn profiles.[48]

Whew! That's quite a busy day! This digital obsession helps to explain the findings of one jaw-dropping survey: One in three smartphone owners would rather give up sex than their phones![49]

The new omnichannel consumer who seems to be always on, and who receives input from many different sources, is a mixed blessing for marketers. On the one hand, companies no longer control where customers find and evaluate their alternatives. Today it's more about trying to be everywhere, or at least at the stops you know consumers routinely make on their journeys. On the other hand, there's a lot to be said for having an engaged consumer who proactively searches for the latest news about a range of products and services s/he may purchase in the next 15 minutes or in the next 15 months. Thus it's vital for marketers to learn more about: "When does my customer's problem become my opportunity?"

As we "bowl together" more often, the fundamental nature of the decision-making process shifts from a solo journey to a group experience. We know from 75 years of research that the (perceived) presence of others exerts a huge influence on an individual's choices. Classic studies like "The Milgram Experiment," that induced ordinary people into delivering severe electric shocks when the experimenter pressured them, chillingly illustrate what peer pressure can push a person to do. Although the selection of a dress, tablet or car may not seem like the kind of life-or-death decision that people make in psychology experiments, approval or censure by a consumer's "hive" can seem almost as dire in the moment.

In addition to the compulsion to conform, we know that a person's tolerance for risk changes when s/he is part of a group. In many cases we observe what social psychologists call a *risky shift*. This means that individuals tend to choose a riskier option when it's a collective decision than each would make if left to their own devices. The well-documented "risky shift phenomenon" should make retailers sit up and take notice: The purse strings tend to loosen when people shop with others, either online or in stores.

> **GRAB YOUR SLEDGEHAMMER**
> Shoppers behave differently when they're in the company of others. They tend to visit more areas of a store or mall, and their inhibitions about buying some items loosen up. Retailers should think about promotions that reward groups for patronizing their venues. The added ROI will be worth it.

Social Scoring Redux: Fire the Customer!

Is the customer always right? Not anymore. There's another aspect of social scoring, albeit largely overlooked, that has the potential to be a game-changer in retailing and customer service. While we're busily documenting our interactions with salespeople and other service providers, they're returning the favor. People who work in small businesses have always been aware of problem customers who drop in periodically to torment them. But now at least in theory, a salesperson or other service provider at any kind of organization large or small can grade your behavior. And the icing on the cake is that they can share these scores with others. It's no longer only Santa who knows if you've been naughty or nice.

At platforms like Airbnb and Uber, users get a rating each time they patronize the service. It's no surprise that according to Lyft and Uber drivers, failure to leave a tip is a sure-fire road to a dismal evaluation. For your future reference, these are some other behaviors that will make or break a five-star rating straight from the mouths of operators:[50]

- "Don't puke in or ruin the car."
- "The most common reason for a lower passenger rating is making us wait after we arrive to pick you up. If you're ready to go at the curb when we arrive, it means a lot."
- "Rude passengers immediately get four stars. Depending on the level of rudeness, their rating can go down to one star."
- "Passengers get a one-star ding for everything they mess up, like not being ready, slamming doors, or being impolite."
- "I will deduct points for rude behavior or illegal activities. I will also deduct points for passengers who leave garbage in my car."

This is not just FYI stuff; a bad rating can prevent you from booking rooms or rides down the road. Uber and Lyft share rider ratings with other drivers, who may choose not to pick up a passenger with an unsavory record. Open Table bans people from using its service if they have missed too many reservations. At Airbnb, you sometimes have to make the case for your worthiness to stay at a guesthouse. The application process feels a bit like getting a surprise inspection visit from a social worker when you're trying to adopt a child.

This transparency may disrupt not only the service economy – it also can obliterate the traditional power disparity between buyer and seller. Suddenly, the user has to play nice and think about how today's nasty behavior will influence tomorrow's reputation.

So far it doesn't seem that service businesses have thought much about the potential impact of this reverse rating process, but it could be just a matter of time before overly demanding patients need to locate doctors who will agree to put up with them, customers who like to yell at repairmen have no one to fix their leading toilets, and perhaps even students who email their professor at 2:00 a.m. with urgent questions about assignments that were due two weeks ago get banned from registering for classes (OK, that last one is a fantasy of mine that I just threw in there). We are just beginning to feel the rumblings of this wall coming down, but it could be a big one.

The ability of sharing economy hosts to rate their guests threatens to upend our bedrock assumption that "the customer is always right."

GRAB YOUR SLEDGEHAMMER

Will the shoe be on the other foot? We may only be scratching the tip of the iceberg here. Imagine when new services arise that aggregate customers' ratings across platforms and sell that data to companies. Ironically, consumers may have to woo providers, just as businesses court customers today. As customer rating services start to take off, both parties to a transaction will feel more pressure to behave or deliver good service. This kind of social scoring is still in early days, and the focus thus far has been exclusively on identifying "problem children."

That's fine, but what about a more positive take? Reward consumers who bring home a good report card! Depending on your business, there are various metrics you can use – complaining behavior, credit scores, frequency of product returns, etc. You'll build a bond and also help to maximize the proportion of your customer base that acts responsibly.

The Hive Still Needs Queen Bees: We Call Them Curators

According to one estimate, the average human brain receives about 34 Gb of information per day. That's enough to overwhelm a laptop within a week.[51] We saw earlier that hyperchoice is not a good thing, because the quality of our decisions diminishes when there are just too many options.

The futurist Stewart Brand famously observed, "information wants to be free," in defense of an unfettered Internet. However, what's not as well-known is that he went on to say, "information [also] wants to be expensive," because it's so valuable.[52] The paradox he was noting is that the value of all this amazing content is lost if we can't use it.

As the amount of information available to all of us cascades, the need for editors, curators, gatekeepers, whatever you'd like to call them, to sift the wheat from the chaff grows as well. The hive mind can be overwhelmed by a surplus of choices. Sure, information wants to be free – but anarchy just doesn't work when you're trying to find that perfect outfit.

What does this mean for marketers? Very simply, *content curation* is as, or more important, than *content creation*.

Still, it's the creation aspect that fixates most professionals right now. The two-way interactivity of Web 2.0 transformed an entire generation of passive Internet consumers into proactive Internet producers. These amateur content creators upload vast amounts of "stuff" 24/7. Today almost anyone can film their own commercial for a favorite product, or even worse upload a diatribe or parody of a brand they don't like.

This opening of the dikes worries a lot of people in the advertising business. They see the tidal wave of consumer-generated content that's about to engulf them, and fret that they'll be out of a job very soon. Who needs copywriters and art directors, when amateurs can shoot their own crowd-pleasing commercial that logs thousands of views on You Tube?

Doritos' success with this new amateur model shows why the pros are worried. The brand's crowdsourced "Crash the Super Bowl" initiative was a huge win during its ten year run. This campaign allowed individuals to submit their own Doritos commercials. The winning spots aired during precious ad time at the Super Bowl, the Mecca of broadcast advertising.

Why worry about juvenile spots filmed by novices on shoestring budgets? Very simple – the winning spots earned top-five rankings on the *USA Today* Ad Meter every year in which they aired, and they claimed the #1 ranking four times.

But take a deep breath: Even a campaign like "Crash the Super Bowl" required the input of many professionals, who helped to find the few pearls in the thousands of oysters that everyday people submitted to the contest. As the CMO of the National Football League noted about the Doritos spots:

One reason that crowdsourcing is no longer as threatening to agencies is because shops still play a role.... You still need people to organize it. Crash didn't happen because consumers decided to do it. This program happened because somebody had the idea, organized it, made it happen, provided the vehicles.... The agency world is as relevant as ever, if not arguably more relevant, as more crowdsourced individual ideas have come to pass.[53]

The upshot: Marketing professionals don't make all the rules any longer, but you still get to decide who plays the game. The tsunami of information every consumer faces creates the need for individuals and organizations to filter out 99% of the noise (on a good day). Like it or not, there's a lot of mind-numbing stuff out there, and even the most brain-dead among us can look at only so many cute kitty videos.

This curation function is golden to consumers who are desperate to simplify their lives. Lifestyle gurus preach the virtues of decluttering. Countless articles and YouTube videos demonstrate "hacks" or shortcuts to minimize the time we spend on our to-do lists. Magazines and blogs publish "Top 10 lists" of the best restaurants, employers, roller coasters, and just about anything else you can imagine. Ironically, as our access to better and better data about our lives increases, so too does our need for editors to make sense of all of it.

It Takes a Village to Cut a Record

Sociologists refer to the set of individuals and organizations that create and market a cultural product such as a record album, a movie, a shoe style, or a football game as a *culture production system (CPS).* The structure of a CPS determines the types of products it creates. Factors such as the number and diversity of competing systems influence the selection of products from which we choose at any point in time. For example, an analysis of the country/western music industry showed that the hit records it produces are similar to one another when a few large companies dominate the industry, but when a greater number of labels compete we see more diversity in musical styles.[54]

A culture production system has three major subsystems:

1. A *creative subsystem* to generate new symbols and products

2. A *managerial subsystem* to select, make tangible, produce, and manage the distribution of new symbols and products

3. A *communications subsystem* to give meaning to the new product and provide it with a symbolic set of attributes

An example of the three components of a culture production system for a music release is (1) a singer (e.g., Beyoncé, a creative subsystem); (2) a company (e.g., Columbia Records distributes Beyoncé's CDs so it's a managerial subsystem); and (3) the advertising agencies and corporations that promote the product as a communications subsystem (e.g., PepsiCo works with Beyoncé's company Parkwood Entertainment to promote her music and arrange for her appearances in venues including the Super Bowl and even on a limited edition set of Pepsi soda cans).[55]

As we know all too well, not all cultural products succeed. In fact, the large majority never makes it past the cutting room floor. Indeed it's literally impossible for every clothing label, new album, potato chip flavor, or lamp design to thrive. Consumers simply don't have the time, bandwidth or money to buy everything that gets thrown at them (much as some may valiantly try). They need agents in the system to winnow down the options for them, lest the hyperchoice tsunami sweeps over them. Think of this vast ocean of options pouring into a giant funnel – only a (relatively) small proportion of these choices trickle out at the other end for shoppers to consider.

The need for these gatekeepers illustrates why, for example, amateur bloggers have become such a force to be reckoned with in industries as diverse as apparel, tech products and wine. Contrary to what some observers proclaim, we still need "experts" to sift through the ocean of options for us. What has changed is that the potential pool of expertise no longer is confined to the people and institutions, such as "intellectual elites" (unfortunately perhaps including college professors) and legacy publications like *Vogue* that traditionally held the reins of power.

Fig. 172.—Magic Funnel.

Cultural products such as music, clothing, literature, movies, and yes, even science represent a very small subset of the possibilities that are vetted by agents of culture production systems.

Ding ding ding! That's where marketing agents enter to provide value. *Many cultural gatekeepers* or *tastemakers* have a big say in the products we consider. They filter the overflow of information as it travels down the "funnel." Gatekeepers include movie, restaurant, and car reviewers; interior designers; disc jockeys; retail buyers; magazine editors; and increasingly a fan base that obsessively follows and shares the latest gossip, styles, TV and film plots, and other pieces of popular culture. Sociologists call this set of agents the *throughput sector*.[56]

Cultural gatekeepers decide which products get to compete for consumers' attention.

But here's a twist: Today many of the new gatekeepers are algorithms, as AI (artificial intelligence) applications take center stage to sift through reams of data and recommend choices to us. For example, startups like Mezi and Hello Hipmunk learn clients' preferences over time, so they can customize travel recommendations for picky vacationers.[57]

This sea change presents both a challenge to traditional centers of expertise and a golden opportunity to newcomers. Today there is huge market value in *credentialing*, i.e. demonstrating that according to some standard one is in fact eligible to opine on the "correct" clothing styles, the best wines, the most cutting-edge tech, etc.

One illustration of this battle for credibility is the trend toward the awarding of *microdegrees* (or *nanodegrees*) in the tech space. These credentials, offered by online education disruptors such as Coursera and Udacity, do an end run around legacy higher ed agents in the CPS. Microdegrees certify expertise in a specific skill set that employers desire without the price tag of an entire degree program.[58]

Similar "guild issues" regarding the consensus about who is an expert – and thus qualified to curate consumers' choices -- are roiling fields as diverse as physical conditioning (e.g. the National Strength and Conditioning Association versus "upstart" regimens like CrossFit), psychiatrists versus social workers, and even the right of Orthodox rabbis versus those in other branches of Judaism to certify who is a Jew. There will be winners and losers for sure, but we can count on a growing demand for agents to provide these services – and many opportunities wait for companies that recognize this need and move to fill the gaps in this growing market.

GRAB YOUR SLEDGEHAMMER

The democratization of the Internet ironically amplifies the need for professionals to select and curate worthy content. That's why it's important to appreciate the role YOU play in the vast marketplace ecosystem. While no single designer, company, or advertising agency creates popular culture, each has a role to play and adds value to what end consumers wind up wearing, listening to, reading, eating, and driving. Opportunities abound in virtually every vertical for intermediaries who assume the role of curator. Consumers crave simplification, and they're willing to pay a premium for services that separate the wheat from the chaff.

End users also want to demonstrate that they are able to distinguish between a silk purse and a sow's ear, so there's also a huge market for credentialing services that provide nanodegrees focused on very specific skill sets. We are slowly moving away from the one-size-fits-all degree model. The new one gives students of all stripes *a la carte* options to customize a resumé with a collection of "badges" that signal proficiency in very specific competencies, whether computer coding, SEO or film editing.

Social Shopping

The massive need for curation in marketplaces brings us back full circle to the obituary for traditional, linear decision making. The early years of e-commerce cast doubt on the viability of the online channel, because clicking at home on a computer can't replicate the experience of trying on an item, receiving feedback from shopping partners, or even the thrill of wearing the new garment home.

Will the always-on consumer kill the process of linear decision making?

That criticism is almost moot today, and it likely will be ancient history within a few years. New technologies are coming to the fore that marry the convenience of online shopping with the "warm and fuzzy" experience of shopping with your BFF in a fancy store. These applications bridge the gap between digital and IRL (in real life) in several ways:[59]

- *Scrapbooking sites* like vi.sualize.us, Polyvore and Pinterest allow shoppers to collect a bunch of options as they surf the web, just as an in-store shopper might accumulate a pile of pants to lug into the dressing room. Members of the community submit their outfit ideas for others to use.

- *Virtual try-on sites* like StyleWhile, My Virtual Model and Joy of Clothes allow shoppers to superimpose outfits over a photo or avatar of themselves. In some cases the user can customize the model's body dimensions to yield a more accurate representation.

- *Pre-purchase feedback sites* like Motilo and Instagram solicit reactions from a user's social network and other *fashionistas*.

- *Recommendation sites* like ClosetSpace and Cladwell consider variables such as weather and occasion to generate suggestions for outfits the user can purchase on sponsoring websites.

- *Augmented reality* applications create an immersive, interactive experience either at home or in-store. Companies including Converse, Uniqlo, and IKEA have successfully deployed AR platforms that enhance the bricks-and-mortar customer experience.

Recommendation engines drive e-commerce upselling.

Madison's prom shopping experience incorporated some of this new tech. Recall that she created her own personal virtual model to try on dresses. Now compare this process to the "old days" of picking items out of an online catalog without having any idea of what they would actually look like when they arrived. Madison also shared photos of dresses with her friends online, and she didn't make a move until they weighed in on each. Just as her mom Mary was able to audition her choices in front of her three friends in a store dressing room, Madison now accesses others' feedback before rather than after the sale. Same task, different ZMOT.

Let's refer to these emerging platforms collectively as *social shopping*. They allow an online customer to simulate the experience of shopping in a bricks-and-mortar store. Even though she may be sitting on a bus or lounging at home in her PJs, she can access feedback from other people either prior to or after she decides on a purchase. Social shopping is a hybrid of social networking and online retailing. As technology continues to mature, social shopping may even offer a more compelling purchase experience than the in-store interactions it replaces. In the process, it may transform the shopping experience as we currently understand it.

Maybe it's time for marketers to go shopping as well – for new models that explain the wild, wild world of today's nonlinear, always on decision maker.

WALL #3: Offline vs. Online

The grandparent's lament: My three lovely little granddaughters live in L.A., while we live in Philadelphia. That makes regular visits to spoil them a bit difficult. However, my wife and I often "Face Time," so they are quite used to seeing us onscreen. That's certainly a different experience from the disembodied voice I heard over the phone every now and then, when I was growing up far away from my own grandparents. I'm guessing that especially when they were very young, my little darlings didn't make such a sharp distinction between the smiling faces they saw onscreen versus the ones that occasionally dropped into their living room.

We used to "go online" and then return to the physical world, perhaps several times a day. Today's *Digital Natives* seamlessly cross the boundaries between offline and online, pretty much all day and all night. Often they inhabit both spaces at once; they multitask while they watch TV, post on Facebook, listen to streaming music, and occasionally even do their homework. <u>They don't regard their physical and digital personas as separate identities</u>. There no longer is a wall that stands between our offline and online selves.

Kids no longer "go online" – they live online.

As e-commerce began to take off, many retailers fretted that physical stores would soon be consigned to museums. The discussion evolved from determining whether a store should branch into e-commerce, to how much time and money to devote to e-commerce versus bricks-and-mortar, to whether e-commerce activity would cannibalize bricks-and-mortar sales.

For a variety of reasons, we can use 20/20 hindsight to state that bricks-and-mortar is safe – at least for the time being. For one thing, physical stores still attract more traffic and are more profitable. For another, younger shoppers actually prefer them by a wide margin to digital options (even though they may eventually order the merchandise online).[60]

But my point here makes that beside the point. The new hybrid consumer renders the bricks-and-mortar versus e-commerce debate obsolete. It no longer makes sense to draw a line between offline and online shopping (or dating, learning and many other activities). Simply put, most of us no longer "go" online. We are online all day and sometimes all night, just as we are offline for much of the same time.

The ability to seamlessly transition back and forth, back and forth, between the physical and digital worlds is a hallmark of today's technological environment. Just ask any professor who tries to deliver in-class lectures as his students listen with one ear while they check their social media posts. Intel refers to these digital expansions of our literal, physical existence as *connected visual computing*. I simply view it as a challenge to see what I can possibly do to get my students to look up from their devices. Tap dancing and serving free beer have been considered.

Those who were around way back in the 20th century (many of my undergrads weren't!) have bittersweet memories of laboriously dialing into the Internet and waiting patiently for a page to load. Back in those days, we viewed a company that printed a URL in ads to show it actually had a website as cutting-edge. Broadband of course changed that. Today for most of us (the huge social class and income gap in access notwithstanding), being online has morphed from a luxury to a necessity. Teens now spend over nine hours a day on social media platforms – and during 60% of that time they are connecting on mobile devices.

The rest of us still log a respectable amount of time – the average adult devotes almost two hours to social media everyday, which translates to a total of 5 years and 4 months spent over a lifetime. For what it's worth, you can fly to the moon and back 32 times in the same time, or if you prefer walk your dog about 93,000 times (probably while you listen to XM Radio on your smartphone).

We still put in more time in front of the Boob Tube (an average of 7 years and 8 months watching TV in a lifetime), but given current trajectories it won't be long before social media overtakes television (especially as more cord cutters actually consume their TV content on mobile devices).[61] And, these figures don't include the time we spend on e-commerce sites, Wikipedia, or other informational or transactional websites.

Instead of thinking about offline/online as an either/or dichotomy, let's get with the program and paint a more realistic picture: Visualize a consumer who spends a typical day moving in and out of these environments – and often existing simultaneously within them. Then our job is to better understand what these consumer experiences look like, and to think carefully about how to deploy our resources to be sure our brand is adequately represented wherever our customer happens to be at any given time.

If we can adjust our thinking a bit, we'll be following the lead of some of the most successful digital companies on the planet. Three recent strategic acquisitions make it look pretty obvious how these organizations think about the future:

- Minecraft is a hugely popular Swedish online gaming site. Microsoft paid $2.5 billion for the site.

- Twitch is a live video-game-streaming site with more than 55 million users that's like a YouTube for video games. Amazon paid $970 million for it (in cash, thank you).

- Oculus VR is a startup that makes virtual reality headsets. Facebook shelled out $2 billion for the company.

In addition to rocking the worlds of some very happy entrepreneurs with these huge paydays, these purchases provide a strong hint of how our worlds as consumers are going to change as well. Each deal indicates how these companies plan to expand and transform our connections to digital environments as they add rich new visual interfaces.

From Offline to Online

In 2009, director James Cameron's hit movie *Avatar* popularized the idea of humans who could take on the appearance of another life form and exist in a different world (in this case, a 10 foot tall blue humanoid who lives on the planet Pandora). *Avatar* is a Hindu word that means a manifestation of a deity or released soul in bodily form on earth, but in the computing world it refers to a digital representation of a person.

Well before the movie's release, it turns out that millions of people around the world were already creating avatars and spending countless hours in alternative worlds right here on Earth. Indeed, way back in 2006 *Business Week* ran a cover story about so-called *virtual worlds* like Second Life. The article highlighted the amount of real money players were making as they bought and sold virtual items to dress their avatars and furnish their digital residences.

Second Life generated $500 million in that year alone, and many major marketing organizations including Apple, H&R Block and Reebok set up advertising or retailing operations in this virtual world.[62] We even saw some limited success when firms used these worlds for marketing research to test store layouts and develop new products. For example, Starwood's Aloft hotel brand prototyped the design of its public spaces in Second Life and used feedback from avatar guests to modify its blueprints in the real world.[63]

A screenshot from a virtual Saint Joseph's University campus my colleague Natalie Wood and I created in Second Life. Immersive digital interfaces are profoundly transforming the educational space, as students from around the world can participate in virtual classrooms together in real time.

The allure of virtual worlds such as Second Life, Kaneva, Whyville, Habbo and others has faded; especially as new virtual reality technologies begin to surface (more on this shortly). However, even today many popular virtual worlds especially targeted to kids and tweens abound, such as Poptropica, Toontown and Binweevils. The Japanese never gave up on this format, and there are several popular erotic virtual worlds based on *manga* characters -- virtual porn is here to stay. More prosaically here at home, Linden Labs, the creator of Second Life, launched its new Sansar platform in 2017 to enable developers to create and monetize their own virtual worlds.[64]

Virtual worlds still hold promise as platforms to facilitate marketing activities as diverse as enterprise training, new product development, trade shows, advertising, and shopping. They are a scalable way to encourage employees and consumers to interact in a non-threatening environment on a global level.

Examples abound, but I'll just share one here. The screenshot below is taken from a virtual world my colleagues and I created for Avon's younger Mark brand. The company has thousands of distributors who have very limited opportunities to interact with one another (unless they pay to attend the raucous annual convention). Sales leaders typically connect with these women online or on a monthly conference call that can include hundreds of participants.

As an alternative that would allow individual distributors to interact one-on-one with others in their region, we built a virtual meeting venue -- complete with Mark's color palette. Each woman entered the room as an avatar. She could talk to other individuals and also watch an audiovisual presentation by Mark's people. Results were very encouraging, to say the least. Many participants told us they really appreciated the opportunity to make a more personal connection with their peers. The typical distributor is relatively young, and usually a novice when it comes to selling or managing a business. It's a huge advantage to network with others who are in the same boat – kind of like a digital version of the Mastermind groups that are all the rage today.[65]

Our virtual distributor meeting venue for Avon's Mark brand.

GRAB YOUR SLEDGEHAMMER

Immersive digital environments present huge opportunities for organizations to create inexpensive, scalable venues that can bring together employees, suppliers, and customers. These platforms have the potential to transform education, enterprise training, trade shows, new product development and customer insights.[66]

Online Gaming

We may not all be aware of virtual worlds, but many of us certainly know a lot about online videogames. By one estimate there are more than two billion (yes, billion) video game players worldwide. While Asia is the epicenter of gaming, here in the U.S. we are pretty well represented. In fact, in about six in 10 American households at least one person plays these games at least three hours per week. And, throw out that tired stereotype of the gamer as a complexion-challenged teenage boy huddled in the basement surrounded by a pile of old pizza boxes. The average game player is 35 years old, and about one quarter are over 50.

It also may come as a surprise that about 40% of these players are female.[67] That explains why mainstream brands including Dunkin Donuts, Mercedes-Benz, Pillsbury, and Huggies actively advertise on these platforms. Marketers like to reach people in these environments, because they feel consumers are more relaxed, happier, and less stressed out when they play mobile games than while they do any other activity on mobile devices.[68] Next to social networking, game play is the most popular reason that consumers use their phones – they average 537 minutes per month in play.

Some traditionalists may view video gaming as anti-social. Perhaps this is because players seem to "get lost" in their own worlds, or because some of the games challenge participants to brutally kill as many "bad guys" as they can. However, the reality is that online gaming is very much a social activity. Games are interactive and typically involve multiple players (sometimes hundreds or even thousands!). There are defined rules of engagement and a community of enthusiasts that encourage one another to keep playing (which helps to explain why revenues from social games are expected to top $2 billion by 2020).[69]

Role-playing games (RPGs) are the epitome of digital social interaction. Whether *Dungeons and Dragons, World of Warcraft, League of Legends* or many others, these games propel players into a fantasy world where each takes on a specific role. And many of these games boast literally millions of players worldwide, earning them the label *MMORGP – Massive Multiplayer Online Role-Playing Games.*

That doesn't count the burgeoning *e-Sports* industry, where rapt spectators watch other people play competitive videogames, often in large stadiums. The fascination with viewing a bunch of gamers manipulate digital warriors on huge screens escapes me personally, but clearly it's seducing a lot of *aficionados*: Revenue this year is projected at $465 million, and the global audience for e-Sports is about 385 million and climbing.[70] Almost overnight, "geeks" with sharp minds and nimble fingers are turning into sports idols, complete with groupies and lucrative endorsement deals.

Especially for "hard-core gamers," these games are anything but – they are an immersive activity that may demand as much time per week as some of us devote to our jobs. Indeed videogame addiction is a growing problem. Experts estimate that between 2-10% of children exhibit signs of this syndrome, where symptoms include:[71]

- Significant interference with school, work, or relationships
- Avoiding other commitments in order to keep playing
- Frequently turning down social invitations in favor of gaming
- Loss of interest in previously enjoyed activities
- Regular gaming "binges" of 8 hours or more nonstop

You Are What You Post

"How do I look?" For many of us, daily life is punctuated by a preoccupation with how we come off to others. Multibillion-dollar industries (obviously) owe their very existence to our need to experiment with and modify appearance. In the immortal words of Charles Revson, the founder of Revlon: "We don't sell lipsticks. We sell dreams."

You don't need to be a supermodel to "manage" the way you appear to others. In fact we all do it every day. If we didn't, we would have no need for mirrors. Sixty years ago, the sociologist Erving Goffman, among others, wrote extensively about the elaborate process of *impression management*. Since that time, volumes of social psychological studies have empirically documented the preening process and the huge impact physical appearance exerts on our judgments of those around us. *Mea culpa*: I published my share of those.

Valuing good-looking people is one of the most pervasive biases around – psychologists refer to it as "the what is beautiful is good" phenomenon. In one recent manifestation, the *BeautifulPeople.com* online dating site literally allows only attractive people to join (you have to have your photo approved by members). Now it's expanding its service to employers who want to hire "good-looking staff." One of the site's managers explains, "Attractive people tend to make a better first impression on clients, win more business and earn more."[72]

For better or worse, he's actually right: One study reported that on average a U.S. worker who was among the bottom one-seventh in looks, as assessed by randomly chosen observers, earned 10 to 15 percent less per year than a similar worker whose looks were assessed in the top one-third—a lifetime difference, in a typical case, of about $230,000.[73] Who says, "Beauty is only skin deep?"

Furthermore, our perceptions of our <u>own</u> attractiveness profoundly influence feelings of self-worth as well. Way back in 1902, the sociologist Charles Horton Cooley wrote about the *looking-glass self* that operates as a sort of psychological sonar: We take readings of our own identity when we "bounce" signals off others and try to predict their impression of us.

Like the distorted mirrors in a funhouse, our appraisal of who we are depends upon whose (imagined) perspectives we take. We also calibrate these sonar readings to the external standards we adopt: Studies show that young women alter their perceptions of their own body shapes and sizes after they watch as little as 30 minutes of TV programming or leaf through the pages of a typical fashion magazine brimming with thin, airbrushed models.

The looking glass self operates as psychological sonar.

It's practically a truism to state that many consumers run on an endless treadmill to live up to standards of appearance the beauty industry promotes. Like the hapless Yossarian in the novel *Catch 22*, it seems that we can never attain quite attain the goal we seek. We get close, but then the ideal changes, and it's back to the trainer and stylist again.

While some claim this is an unfortunate symptom of our modern consumer culture, in reality there <u>always</u> have been idealized standards of beauty for the masses to idolize. Throughout history, cultural elites and rulers meticulously edited the impressions they communicated to their peers and followers. It's hard to imagine that Julius Caesar, George Washington, or the British royal family (past and present) didn't have strong opinions about which of their images would adorn currency or portraiture.

Every society anoints certain men and women as aesthetic ideals, and motivates emulation of these exemplars as it rewards attractive people (however a culture defines this quality). We characterize periods of history by a specific "look," or ideal of beauty. Often these relate to broader cultural trends, such as today's emphasis on fitness and toned bodies.

A look at U.S. history reveals a succession of dominant ideals. For example, in sharp contrast to today's emphasis on health and vigor, in the early 1800s it was fashionable for women to appear delicate to the point of looking ill. The poet John Keats described the ideal female of that time as "…a milk white lamb that bleats for man's protection." Other past looks include the voluptuous, lusty woman that Lillian Russell made popular; the athletic Gibson Girl of the 1890s; and the small, boyish flapper of the 1920s exemplified by the silent movie actress Clara Bow.[74] More recently, Kim Kardashian's ample behind "broke the internet" and inspired legions of young women to sign up for buttocks enhancements due to what one plastic surgeon dubbed "the Kardashian Effect."[75]

Who Sets Beauty Standards? The Elite vs. the Masses

Cultural icons, whether members of the Kardashian clan, Jennifer Aniston, Jennifer Lopez, or Brad Pitt, Ryan Gosling, or Blake Shelton, continue to serve as benchmarks for millions of men and women who dream that they too will someday adorn the cover of *People* magazine. But here's what's different now: It's no longer the cream of society that gets to decide who is hot and who is not. The increasing racial diversity and the exposure of that Internet thing again help to democratize the selection of standard-bearers. For example, in the last twenty years or so the men and women selected by *People* as the "World's Most Beautiful" have become markedly darker in skin tone, and older as well.[76]

Throughout history it's typically been the elites who defined standards of appearance, and the wealthy who had the resources to emulate them. Indeed, the notion that a working class woman could walk into a store and buy a dress rather than making it at home is a fairly recent innovation. Wealthy women traditionally commissioned designers to create one-off styles, which were then copied by other upward-striving consumers (often on their own sewing machines). That's why so-called "designer labels" that are snapped up by the mass market represent a logical contradiction – or at least a bastardization of the original meaning.

Today, all that has changed. The wall between The *Elite vs. The Masses* has come down in terms of the ability to procure apparel, cosmetics, and other status markers. The rise of the so-called *mass class* blurs the distinction between lower and upper classes (at least for everyday purchases). This new stratum of millions of people around the world who are rapidly acquiring impressive buying power brings with it almost unfettered access to the same kinds of products and service providers that only the elite could access in the past.[1] For example, it's not at all uncommon for consumers who bring home fairly low incomes to "splurge" on at least a few expensive trinkets. Of U.S. women with household incomes under $75,000, ¾ own a bauble from Tiffany and 1/3 purchased something from Bulgari.[77]

Professional "identity managers" come in many forms, from hairstylists and cosmetologists to wardrobe consultants and resumé writers. Doctors perform nearly 860,000 cosmetic-surgery procedures in the U.S. each year alone. In some circles nose jobs or breast implants are part of the rite-of-passage for teenage girls, and an increasing number of men spring for pectoral enlargements.

The Digital Self

But back to the crumbling of the offline/online wall: Our wired world takes the process of strategic self-presentation to a new level.[78] We may still need a trained surgeon to reshape a troublesome nose, but we can undertake other makeovers on our own. This is especially true when it comes to the identity we express on digital platforms.

In the old days, a woman might get a "makeover" at a department store, or perhaps sit for a Glamour Shots photo session that temporarily transformed her into a beauty queen (or hooker, depending upon your point-of-view). The late Hugh Hefner owed a big chunk of his fortune to the abilities of his staff who photographed *Playboy*'s centerfolds beginning with Marilyn Monroe in the 1950s. These airbrushed women literally do not exist, at least as they appear in the magazine.

Indeed, in the course of conducting several research studies at major fashion modeling agencies in Manhattan (it's a dirty job, but someone's got

---

[1] Ironically, as I will discuss at the end of this book, the leveling of status markers occurs even as income inequality between higher- and lower-income consumers grows dramatically. The comparisons here apply primarily to relatively low-profile acquisitions, and not to big-ticket items like education or housing.

to do it), I was often struck by the appearance of the various "supermodels" I would encounter in the hallways. Attractive women, to be sure – but nothing close to what they looked like after a photo shoot had gone into "post-production."

Today, techie teenagers can effortlessly produce the same before/after results with Photoshop or even Snapchat filters. Such transformations are possible because we have access to online "post-production" tools that give us the ability to create our own makeovers. These free or inexpensive applications allow virtually anyone to dramatically modify his or her *digital self* at will. We carefully "modify" the profile photos we post on Facebook, or the descriptions we share on online dating sites. Retailers can help us along on the path of self-delusion as well – sometimes it's as simple as adding a slight curvature to a dressing room mirror to make the reflected image look thinner.[79]

Reality vs. Fantasy

With all of the "enhancements" that are available, what happens to the wall that separates *Reality vs. Fantasy*? In Israel, an advertiser must state if it has used any kind of digital editing to create a slimmer model. France just passed a similar measure. For now, let's put aside the rebuttal by industry insiders that this practice is so pervasive that such a law is highly impractical – almost every ad would have to carry a disclaimer! Let's also side-step the more abstract philosophical arguments about how we know that anything is real.

The debate more generally highlights our fundamental tendency to believe that what we see in the media is "real" unless we are otherwise advised – and likewise our tendency to put more stock in what we see than in what we know. The truth is that most of us are quite gullible. And we're quite content to be. We willingly agree to a *suspension of disbelief* any time we attend a live theatre production or watch a television sitcom. During these performances we enter into an unwritten contract with the show's creators to assume that what we see is really happening. Even the current craze for "reality shows" belies the irony that there's very little that's real about them. Contestants are carefully screened, often coached, and sometimes willing to say or do whatever it takes to stand in the media spotlight. Down comes the wall between reality and fantasy.

Welcome to the Metaverse

Way back in 1999, *The Matrix* captivated our imaginations. The movie depicted a future where most humans live in a simulated reality that intelligent machines created. Today as artificial intelligence (AI) applications like IBM's Watson become more sophisticated, the notion that machines will soon run our lives isn't so far-fetched.

Of course this pioneering movie (trilogy, actually) didn't invent the scenario of people who inhabit a digital environment apart from their corporeal bodies. That honor goes to the sci-fi author Neal Stephenson, who developed the *metaverse* concept in his seminal 1992 novel *Snow Crash*. He conceived this as a collective virtual space inhabited by our digital Doppelgängers. Essentially, it's a vision of the future Internet on steroids, where we interact with our "friends" as avatars and live parallel lives in cyberspace. Thus in Stephenson's initial vision, a humble pizza delivery boy in the "meat world" transforms into a sword-wielding hero when he enters the metaverse.

For awhile, it looked as if the growth of virtual worlds like Second Life was going to be the fuel that we needed to propel millions of people into the metaverse. However, today a better bet is the new *virtual reality* (VR) technology that is about to bust loose on the consuming public. VR provides a totally immersive experience that transports the user into an entirely separate 3D environment. The commercially available Oculus headset (that little startup Facebook bought) was just the first step in what promises to be an avalanche of consumer-oriented VR technology from major companies including Samsung, Sony and Google.[80] The apparatus is still a bit clunky, but it's a good bet that before we know it Silicon Valley companies that smell the money will find ways to shrink the tech into our eyeglasses.

VR for now is a solitary experience, where each user steps into an immersive world and interacts with software designed to take him on a perceptual ride. I experienced this literally when I had the opportunity to try a developer's version of the Oculus headset a few years ago: I suddenly found myself sitting in a pretty realistic roller coaster. The scary ride I took, all while sitting at a disk, clearly showed me the future of media experiences.

VR platforms hold a lot of promise for marketers as well as gamers. For example, one VR company created a virtual supermarket for Hershey to measure the impact of various in-store marketing tactics designed to encourage shoppers to throw bags of Kisses and other delights into their carts. Shoppers wore a VR headset and navigated the aisles of a virtual Walmart store. They reacted to different variations of Hershey's product displays that allowed the company to identify specific configurations that increased sales.[81]

Other companies are aggressively entering the VR space: In Australia, eBay launched a virtual Myer department store that allows shoppers to view thousands of products without leaving home. Amazon is exploring the idea of creating virtual stores to sell furniture and home appliances like refrigerators that shoppers are reluctant to buy over the Internet sight unseen. This platform will allow customers to see how the item will look in their homes without the bother of having it delivered.[82]

The band Queen created a 360-degree virtual reality music video remake of its 1975 hit *Bohemian Rhapsody*. Innovators in the music industry see a VR future where bands could essentially jam in a sophisticated chat room with musicians from around the world.

They could stream the performance so they wouldn't have to hire an expensive venue for concerts.[83]

This type of shared experience will move us into a new generation of VR – and closer to Stephenson's original vision of the metaverse. Already, MC Entertainment, the world's largest theater chain, has invested $20 million in a company called Dreamscape Immersive that plans to launch what it calls a "virtual-reality multiplex." Instead of showing movies, these venues will offer a variety of virtual reality experiences. Most importantly, its technology will allow up to six people to explore the same environment at once as they interact with avatars of one another.[84] A baby step toward the metaverse!

From Online to Offline

As we spend more and more of our time in digital reality, it's inevitable that some of the things we do online will return with us when we transition back to offline mode. My colleague Jeremy Bailenson at Stanford refers to this as the *Proteus Effect*; our experiences in virtual environments change the way we think and act after we return to our physical state.[II][85]

When people in a study observed an avatar that looked like them engaging in exercise, for example, they were more likely to boost their level of physical activity in the real world at a later point.[86] In another study, college males who entered the virtual world of Second Life as handsome avatars were more likely to act confidently and assertively when they encountered an attractive female student (a confederate of the experimenter) upon returning to their offline environment.[87]

[II] Proteus was a shape-changing Greek god.

About 135,000 people attend the annual ComicCon gathering in San Diego. Many fans come in costumes that they spend months preparing for the event.[88] They dress up to look like (or to "be") favorite characters from movies, comic books, videogames and virtual worlds. This convention is Ground Zero for the worldwide movement known as *cosplay*. The practice started in earnest in Japan, where dressing as *anime* characters has been part of popular culture for many years.

The early evidence that our virtual encounters shape our "real world" self-concepts present some promising therapeutic and marketing implications. Consider for example the potential to elevate the self-esteem and quality of life of the thousands of disabled people who currently patronize virtual worlds like Second Life at designated gathering spots. When they take the form of an avatar that is able to walk, suddenly individuals who suffer from cerebral palsy and other debilitating conditions in their offline lives can easily talk, flirt, run, and even dance. Or, think about the virtual branding experiences we accumulate during the course of our cyberjourneys; their lasting impact provides yet another reason to take emerging practices like advergaming very seriously.

GRAB YOUR SLEDGEHAMMER

Many businesses simply leave money on the table because they ignore disabled consumers.

Consider this: Disabled people are the largest minority market in the United States. One in five U.S. adults lives with a disability that interferes with daily life.[89] The Census Bureau reports that there are 54 million adults with disabilities who spend almost $200 billion annually, yet companies pay remarkably little attention to the unique needs of this vast group. Fully 11 million U.S. adults have a condition that makes it difficult for them to leave home to shop, so they rely almost exclusively on catalogs and the Internet to purchase products. Many people have limited mobility and are unable to gain easy access to stores, entertainment venues, educational institutions, and other locations. Bodily limitations or disfigurements result in real or imagined stigmatization, so self-concept and interpersonal relationships may be problematic.[90] People who rely on wheelchairs for mobility often encounter barriers when they try to enter stores, move around the aisles, or enter dressing rooms that are too narrow to accommodate a chair. Others have mental illnesses, such as excessive anxiety in public places.

A virtual environment can be a life-changer for a disabled person, a veteran who suffers from PTSD, or anyone whose mobility is impaired in their offline world. Take advantage of virtual technologies that remove the walls keeping these people from interacting with other consumers and with companies. You'll improve a lot of lives, but also your bottom line.

The Merger of Offline and Online: Another Wall Down

Imagine a flight attendant who knows what you want even before you hit that call light. Air New Zealand is issuing its crew headsets that allow them to see *holograms* alongside the physical world. When a flight attendant looks at a passenger, the headset displays personal details including their preferred meal and why they're travelling. The device can display a range of personal details, including how long it's been since the person had their last drink. The airline hopes that staff may even be able to detect a passenger's emotional state from cues including facial expressions or heart rate.[91] This is a novel application of *augmented reality (AR)*.

As sexy as VR sounds, I'm putting my money on AR to make a more meaningful -- and immediate -- impact on the way marketers connect with customers.

The term *augmented reality* refers to media that superimpose one or more digital layers of data, images, or video over a physical object. Although I've been touting the benefits of AR to marketers for years (mostly to puzzled gazes), it's been a lot easier to make this point since the explosion of the Pokémon Go fad last summer. Suddenly everyone seems to "get" how AR works when it relates to finding furry creatures that lurk in familiar places. But you don't even have to know how to use your smartphone to launch a Poké Ball in order to grasp the power of AR: If you've seen that yellow line in an NFL game that shows the first down marker, you've also encountered AR in a simple form (hint: that line doesn't actually exist on the field).

Augmented reality (AR) is poised to transform the way we interact with customers. IKEA has been an early mover.

Over the next few years you'll experience AR through your smartphone or tablet. New apps like Google Goggles (for Android phones) and Layar (for Android and Apple devices) impose a layer of words and pictures on whatever you see in your phone's viewer. The Microsoft HoloLens technology that Air New Zealand uses blends holograms with what you see in your physical space so that you can actually manipulate digital images. Thus a user who wants to assemble a piece of furniture or fix a broken sink can actually "see" where each part connects to the next through his or her goggles.[92]

Augmented reality apps open new worlds of information -- and have the potential to revolutionize marketing communications. Would you like to know more about the singer you saw on a CD cover? Or maybe who painted that cool mural in your local bar? How much did that house you were looking at last month actually sell for? Just point your smartphone at each and the information will be superimposed on your screen.[93] AR is about to be big business: Analysts project that revenue from augmented reality apps will hit $5.2 billion.[94]

GRAB YOUR SLEDGEHAMMER

It's hard to oversell the promise of AR for a range of marketing applications. For one, think about your package as a true sales tool. A mascara box can morph into a tutorial about how to apply the makeup. A pill bottle can bring up a physician who walks you through potentially harmful interactions with your other prescriptions. A box of linguini shows you how to use the contents to prepare the best scampi your family has ever tasted. The cover of a romance novel sitting on the shelf at Barnes & Noble gives you a 20 second video teaser about the torrid love affair you'll read about on the pages inside. And so on.

No matter what business you're in (profit or non-profit), put on your AR lenses – and never look at a static, boring surface the same way again.

Facebook CEO Mark Zuckerberg said that he thinks AR could replace anything in your life with a screen, including your TV. Even sooner than that, many tech experts think AR could one day replace your smartphone. After all, why carry a separate phone if your e-mails, texts, calls, and spreadsheets are projected straight into your field of view?[95]

The offline and online worlds have never been closer neighbors.

WALL #4:
Producer vs. Consumer

When the founder of the beauty website *Into the Gloss* decided to create a new cosmetics line, she didn't contact vendors or post ads to entice new buyers. Instead she created an Instagram account — @glossier— and waited for suggestions to flood in. She mined the posts her followers submitted as she developed the line.[96] Thousands of cosmetics *aficionados* helped her to build the new company.

We used to purchase goods and services from professional artisans and manufacturers. Today it's also everyday consumers who produce media content, design products, and invest in startups -- not to mention those who also act as retailers, food critics, tour guides, and even taxi drivers. *Consumer-generated content (CGC)* wipes out the traditional wall between producer and consumer. Everyday people collaborate with, or even replace, professionals in virtually every traditional marketing function. Let's take a look at the most important ones.

Product Development

DeWALT has an insight community of over 10,000 tool users who submit ideas for new products. LEGO fans can join LEGO Ideas, an online community where members submit their own designs for new sets. They vote on submissions – if a project gets 10,000 votes, LEGO considers it for an official LEGO Ideas set it will sell around the world. Similarly, the British furniture company Made.com hosts an annual online contest, where budding new designers submit their work for other designers and customers to vote on. The company produces winning designs within a year, and pays royalties to the winning applicants.[97]

Co-Creation is Here!

Call it *co-creation*, call it *collaborative innovation*, call it *crowdsourcing*: The recruitment of consumers to act as product designers is a growing trend. While this teamwork can be threatening to highly trained designers who fear they will be replaced by hordes of *naïfs*, the less insecure ones recognize that user feedback can only improve upon what they think people want.

The practice of handing the inmates the keys to the asylum is booming. If you're doing this already, be sure to 'fess up about where these innovations come from. That's not just ethical practice; it turns out that buyers actually prefer products users actually suggested. One study that looked at items the Japanese consumer products company Muji sells found that crowdsourced products sold up to 20% more when they were specifically labeled as originating with customers.[98] This helps to explain why some brands are going out of their way to trumpet this co-creation process. The German company Red Chili that sells gear for rock climbers proclaims, "Only climbers know what climbers need."[99]

The co-creation model really made its mark in fashion following the success of the Threadless platform, where aspiring designers submit ideas that the community votes on.[100] The company only produces the winning designs that people say they intend to buy, which virtually assures that inventory will always sell out. Now other co-creation platforms are jumping on the bandwagon, including Polyvore, Krush and of course the thousands of fashion accounts on Instagram.

None of Us is as Smart as All of Us

The crowdsourcing movement picked up steam with the 2004 publication of James Surowiecki's book, *The Wisdom of Crowds*.[101] The author notes that certain conditions must be met for large crowds to make wiser decisions than the individuals within the group (e.g. a diversity of opinions is super helpful). With this *caveat* in mind, the crowdsourcing model has been applied in contexts ranging from political forecasting, to predicting the success of Hollywood movies (the Hollywood Stock Exchange), to new product development by large firms such as major pharmaceutical companies.

These forums, known as *prediction markets*, typically ask participants to "put skin in the game" by rewarding them for correct choices (much like a stock market) rather than for making politically correct or "safe" choices.[102] This approach is best-known as a reliable predictor of political contests, including presidential elections. Oops, the renowned Iowa Electronic Markets predicted a Hillary Clinton win just like everyone else, but otherwise this prediction market has performed remarkably well for many years.[103]

In a prediction market framework, companies from Microsoft to Eli Lilly and Hewlett-Packard empower their employees as "traders." Like a stock market, traders place bets on what they think will happen regarding future sales, the success of new products, or how other firms in a distribution channel will behave. Players often receive a cash reward if their "stock picks" pan out. For example, the pharmaceutical giant Eli Lilly routinely places multimillion-dollar bets on drug candidates that face overwhelming odds of failure. The relatively few new compounds that do succeed have to make enough money to cover the losses the others incur. Obviously, the company will benefit if it can separate the winners from the losers earlier in the process. Lilly ran an experiment in which about 50 of its employees involved in drug development, including chemists, biologists, and project managers, traded six mock drug candidates through an internal market. The group correctly predicted the three most successful drugs.[104]

GRAB YOUR SLEDGEHAMMER

Sad, but true: Many organizations ignore one of the best resources out there for customer insights and forecasting the success of new products: Their own employees.

However, if you do decide to take advantage of this fount of knowledge, it's often counter-productive to simply ask members of different teams to predict whether their own initiatives will succeed. For obvious reasons, these folks often have a vested interest in plugging what they happen to work on.

A prediction market dilutes that bias because it is anonymous, and because it allows employees to put their money where their mouths are. When the participant is rewarded (ideally, financially) if predictions turn out to be accurate, it's much easier to set aside biases and vote for what you really <u>believe</u> will happen rather than what is politically correct or self-serving.

The Maker Movement

The rapidly growing *DIY (do it yourself)* trend represents another way that the wall between producers and consumers is crumbling. Analysts project that this market will grow by about 6% per year over the next several years. When an end user undertakes a DIY project, as the name suggests he or she forsakes help from (or payment to) a third party to make it happen.[105]

The DIY craze is part of a larger trend some call the *Maker's Movement*. A *makerspace* is a collaborative workspace inside a school, library or separate public/private facility for creating, learning, exploring, and sharing. As part of this movement amateurs learn about electronics, 3D modeling and printing, 3D modeling, coding, and robotics, in addition to low-tech skills like woodworking.

Typically a healthy dose of entrepreneurship gets thrown in as well, as makerspaces double as incubators for business startups. Some spaces such as TechShop are themselves turning into businesses as they expand the number of locations where DIYers can access their sophisticated tools for a modest membership fee. Makerspaces already are pouring out success stories, such as the DODOcase company that uses a space in San Francisco to build its popular line of covers for phones and laptops.[106]

Makerspaces turn consumers into product designers and manufacturers.

"Artisanal fries with that?"

Artisanal cheese. Artisanal soap. Artisanal beer. The term is everywhere. It implies that an item isn't mass-produced, and often the maker is a skilled artist who otherwise is "one of us" (i.e., s/he hasn't sold out to a big corporation). The e-commerce site Etsy calls itself "the most beautiful marketplace in the world," and features thousands of unique creations that everyday people sell.

What's feeding the artisanal frenzy? Simply, the quest for authenticity. Consumers today often want to know a product's *provenance*; just where the things they buy came from. The J. Peterman Company clothing catalogs tell stories about the apparel they sell, and upscale grocery stores like Whole Foods provide great detail about the specific farms where produce and meat were raised. I recently ate at a restaurant where the menu actually listed the name of the specific fisherman who caught the catch of the day! *Product genealogy*, or the thirst to trace the backstory of a product from raw materials to final form, is a popular activity for many.

Authenticity is now a key driver of purchase decisions in many categories, whether food, art or fashion. Researchers claim that although authenticity can be a hard concept to pin down, it's generally composed of three attributes: heritage, sincerity, and commitment to quality.[107]

Many companies like to tout their "authentic" story. New Balance describes its Maine factory like this: "Built in 1945, the Depot Street building is the workplace of almost 400 associates. Each pair of shoes they produce is a proud work of craftsmanship that carries a little bit of the long history that is the town and its people."[108]

GRAB YOUR SLEDGEHAMMER

Consumers crave authenticity. They love companies that can boast of a long heritage and a history of giving back to the communities where they operate.

If your company has a backstory, tell it. Often.

Advertising and PR

As we saw earlier, Doritos' hugely successful "Crash the Super Bowl" ad campaign that ran for 10 Super Bowls probably contributed to sleepless nights for many advertising executives who feared for their jobs. The airing of commercials rank amateurs produced – often on a shoestring -- put the crowdsourcing of advertising on the map.

A 2013 *Harvard Business Review* article carried the ominous title, "The End of Traditional Ad Agencies,"[109] as it trumpeted the ascendance of the crowdsourcing model. This obituary is a bit premature, but the inclusion of consumers into a secretive creative process does show how the business is changing now that the wall between advertising creatives and creative amateurs is being dismantled.

Perhaps the bigger story is the content that people create on their own and share directly with others, as opposed to submitting concepts or actual executions to agencies. While a lot of this stuff just provides new takes on dancing cats and other mindless fodder for procrastination, a good chunk advocates or disses specific products and services. Fifty-four percent of adult Internet users regularly create and share photos and videos.[110] The rest of us watch this content, and we use it to help us to decide what to buy and what to shun. The simple reason is that CGC has a lot more "street cred" than paid advertising.

New survey data from 4500 active social media users in the U.S. and Europe found that only 6% of people trust traditional advertising, while over three-quarters prefer to look at user-generated images than the ones they see in professional executions. What's more, photos that feature "real people" are trusted seven times more than the pictures people see in traditional advertising. Furthermore, over half of the respondents said they are more likely to click on an ad that features a user-generated photo, and the same amount are more inclined to buy the product after they see this kind of ad.

Top brands are taking note of the many consumers who enthusiastically recommend their favorite products on social media. Many now use branded hash tags to increase visibility and engagement. Following NYX's #NYXCosmetics campaign, for instance, the company found that customers who interact with UGC have a 93 percent higher average order value and convert to customers at a rate 320 percent higher than those who do not.[111]

15 Minutes of Fame? Try 15 Seconds

To further blur the line between producers and consumers, consider the legions of everyday folks who turn themselves into online celebrities when their commentary and advice about products goes viral. There's little doubt that these consumers' verdicts about what is hot and what is not rule the day, even when compared to expensive endorsements from established stars companies pay (handsomely) to tout their goods and services. According to one study, nearly nine in 10 consumers (84%) make purchases after they read about a product or service on a blog. Among consumers between the ages of 18-34, blogs ranked as the most important source of information to make buying decisions.[112]

While the messages are impactful, the messengers are expendable. In the vast majority of cases fame is fleeting, to put it mildly. The spotlight may shine on a self-made celeb for days, weeks or months when s/he achieves the *microfame* that bloggers like Perez Hilton and the buxom singer Tila Tequila found. They are the lucky ones: Some analysts propose that microfame has morphed into *nanofame* as the glare of the Internet spotlight shines brighter and increasingly faster and we cycle through these celeb wannabees at dizzying speed. Here today, gone today.

What is Reality? Fake Vs. Authentic

Fake news. It seems like it's everywhere. Maybe the blizzard of charges and countercharges about what is real information contributes to our longing for authenticity. For some, the fake news label applies to anything about which they disagree. For others, it's about deliberate manipulations by foreign agents that seek to influence elections or other events.

A similar problem lies with the use of misleading data by companies: *Greenwashing* describes the practice of making false or exaggerated claims about the environmental friendliness of supposedly "green" products. According to one report, more than 95 percent of consumer companies that market as "green" make misleading or inaccurate claims.[113] Fake advertising poisons the well for everyone.

Whatever drives this phenomenon, the wall between fake and authentic content is crumbling quickly. So is consumers' willingness to believe what companies tell them. According to one survey, only 4% of Americans think the marketing industry behaves with integrity, and nearly half of consumers surveyed say they don't trust any news source.[114] Houston, we have a problem.

News platforms are taking steps to rejuvenate their reputations, though with questionable results. Facebook, Twitter and Google each introduced a *trust indicator* on their sites to rebuild readers' faith in the veracity of stories.[115] On Facebook, a tiny "i" icon next to articles on the News Feed will now include more information about the media outlet behind that story.[116]

Reality vs. Mythology

In a more innocent way, marketing communications have blurred the line between reality and fantasy for many years – "Yes, Virginia There is a Santa Claus." Modern day "reality shows" are only the latest media inventions of scripted, fake depictions that purport to be "real." Today's consumer is hard-pressed to point to the reality that underlies celebrities' backstories. Many famous actors change their names as they rewrite their histories: The all-American icon Ralph Lauren used to be Ralph Lifshitz, the son of a Jewish house painter who grew up in Brooklyn. Martha Stewart, another WASP idol, used to be Grace Kostyra - she is 100% Polish.

We almost expect celebs to "embellish" and thus blur the line between reality and the mythology they create. More broadly, much of the information we consume that originates from companies purports to have been born as naturally as Ralph Lauren walks his sheepdogs in The Hamptons. The *content marketing* craze essentially is about creating compelling articles, videos, infographics, podcasts and websites that are so gripping the consumer will forget that the source typically has an axe to grind.[117] The *advertorial* has become an art form that makes a sponsored message look like unbiased and valuable information. In the process, the traditional wall between *Editorial vs. Commercial* content disintegrates.

Perhaps you've heard of the town of Mount Airy in North Carolina near the Virginia border? It was the inspiration for the mythical town of Mayberry in "The Andy Griffith Show." To attract tourists, Mount Airy the real place has slowly transformed itself into the TV town. If you visit the Mayberry Motor Inn, an Aunt Bee look-alike will show you around. You can tour around in a vintage police car like the one that Sheriff Andy Taylor drove (Andy Griffith was born in Mount Airy). If you're lucky you'll stumble upon the actress who played Thelma Lou in the original show; she still signs autographs.[118]

One of the hallmarks of modern advertising is that it creates a condition of *hyperreality*. This refers to the process of making real what is initially simulation or "hype." Advertisers create new relationships between objects and meanings, such as when an ad equates Marlboro cigarettes with the American frontier spirit. In a hyperreal environment, over time it's no longer possible to discern the true relationship between symbol and reality. The "artificial" associations between product symbols and the real world take on lives of their own.

We run into hyperreality a lot lately, because *fandom* has become such a huge force in popular culture. This term refers to communities that form around a media phenomenon like a TV show or movie (e.g. *Lost* or *Star Wars*). Avid (perhaps even obsessed) fans often create products that celebrate made-up "realities." Some recent ones include:

- Pinterest Boards for food mentioned in the steamy novel *Fifty Shades of Gray*

- Cookbooks with "recipes" from the *Mad Men TV series, the Harry Potter movies, Game of Thrones,* and *Downton Abbey*

- T-shirts for fictitious companies like Dunder Mifflin (*The Office*) and the Tyrell Corporation (*Blade Runner*).[119]

- The fictional GEICO gecko "published" a book entitled *You're Only Human: A Guide to Life,* that advises on a range of topics from tattooing to flossing.[120]

GRAB YOUR SLEDGEHAMMER

The wall between truth and lies is crumbling. Consumers don't know whom to trust, other than those in their own social networks (and they could be lying, too). They will value sources that their "friends" sanction – but not necessarily those that link to big companies.

Establish your bona fides within these networks, and the world is your oyster.

Sacred vs. Profane Consumption

Nike recently had to pull a new line of Pro Tattoo Tech Gear clothing line for women after the news came out that the graphics it used came from a sacred Samoan tattoo that only men wear. Consumers started a Change.org petition online and bombarded the brand's Facebook page with negative comments.[121]

Traditional marketing communications erected a big wall between what anthropologists term *Sacred vs. Profane*. *Sacred consumption* occurs when we "set apart" objects and events from normal activities and treat them with respect or awe. Note that in this context the term *sacred* does not necessarily carry a religious meaning, although we do tend to think of religious artifacts and ceremonies as "sacred."

Profane consumption in contrast, describes objects and events that are ordinary or everyday; they don't share the "specialness" of sacred ones. Again, note that in this context we don't equate the word *profane* with obscenity, although the two meanings do share some similarities. In the old days at least, the two domains didn't mix. References to organized religion in the service of selling material goods were traditionally taboo (not counting Xmas sales, perhaps).

Today, this wall has come down. Our pervasive consumer culture imbues many objects, events, and even people with sacred meaning. Many of us regard events such as the Super Bowl and people such as Elvis Presley as sacred. Even the Smithsonian Institution in Washington, DC, maintains a display that features such "sacred items" as the ruby slippers from *The Wizard of Oz*, a phaser from *Star Trek*, and Archie Bunker's chair from the television show *All in the Family*.[122]

As the Smithsonian's collection illustrates, the traditional wall of High Art vs. Low Art also seems to be on the verge of coming down. *High Art* refers to "elite" painting, sculpture, and other works we usually see exhibited only in galleries – conveniently separated from human contact by a wall of glass. In contrast, *Low Art* somewhat condescendingly describes popular culture such as comic books, TV shows and of course advertising that is the province of the masses.[123] When Captain Kirk's weapon is displayed with the same reverence as the Mona Lisa in the Louvre (which in turn is virtually inaccessible these days because of the hordes of tourists who are eager to take a selfie with the tiny masterpiece), we know that things are changing.

We make a similar distinction regarding the wall that separates *Arts vs. Crafts*: An *art product* is an object we admire strictly for its beauty or because it inspires an emotional reaction in us (perhaps bliss, or perhaps disgust). In contrast, we admire a *craft product* because of the beauty with which it performs some function (e.g., a ceramic ashtray or hand-carved fishing lures).[124] A craft tends to follow a formula that permits rapid production.[125]

But clearly the distinction between high and low culture is not as clear as it used to be. In addition to the possible class bias that drives such a distinction (i.e., we assume that the rich have culture but the poor do not), today high and low culture blend together in interesting ways. In addition to the appliances, tires, and cereals it sells by the case, the warehouse club Costco stocks fine art, including limited-edition lithographs by Pablo Picasso, Marc Chagall, and Joan Miró. Paintings by the late artist Thomas Kinkade command large sums, even though they are at least partially created in assembly-line fashion by "Master Highlighters" who embellish each work.

In fact, marketers often invoke high-art imagery to promote products. They may feature works of art on shopping bags or sponsor artistic events to build public goodwill.[126] When observers from Toyota watched customers in luxury car showrooms, the company found that these consumers view a car as an art object. The company then used this theme in an ad for the Lexus with the caption, "Until now, the only fine arts we supported were sculpture, painting, and music."[127]

In addition to sacred objects (whether painted by Rembrandt or Peter Max), we idolize sacred people as we set them apart from the masses. Souvenirs, memorabilia, and even mundane items these celebrities have (supposedly) touched acquire special meanings and lofty price tags. Newspapers pay *paparazzi* hundreds of thousands of dollars for candid shots of stars or royalty. Indeed, many businesses thrive on our desire for products we associate with the famous. There is a flourishing market for celebrity autographs, and objects that celebrities owned, such as Princess Diana's gowns or John Lennon's guitars, sell on eBay for astronomical prices.

The world of sports is sacred to many of us (recent doping and gambling scandals aside). We find the roots of modern sports events in ancient religious rites, such as fertility festivals (e.g., the original Olympics).[128] Teams often join in prayer prior to a game. The sports pages are like the scriptures (and we all know ardent fans who read them "religiously"), the stadium is a house of worship, and the fans are members of the congregation. Devotees engage in observant activities, such as tailgate parties and the synchronized "Wave" in stadiums. The athletes and coaches that fans come to see are godlike; devotees believe they have almost superhuman powers. One study documented more than 600 children whose parents named them after the legendary University of Alabama coach Paul "Bear" Bryant![129]

Tourism is another category of sacred experience. People occupy sacred time and space when they travel on vacation (though you may not think so if you get stuck sleeping on an airport floor because of a plane delay). The tourist searches for "authentic" experiences that differ from his normal world (think of Club Med's motto, "The antidote to civilization").[130] Often, we relax everyday (profane) norms regarding appropriate behavior as tourists, and participate in illicit or adventurous experiences we would never engage in at home ("What happens in Vegas, stays in Vegas").

The other side of the Sacred vs. Profane wall is deteriorating as well. *Desacralization* occurs when we remove a sacred item or symbol from its special place or duplicate it in mass quantities so that it loses its "specialness" and becomes profane. Souvenir reproductions of sacred monuments such as the Washington Monument or the Eiffel Tower, artworks such as the *Mona Lisa* or Michelangelo's *David*, or reproductions of sacred symbols such as the U.S. flag on T-shirts eliminate their special aspects. They become inauthentic commodities with relatively little value.

Religion itself has to some extent become desacralized. Spiritual symbols like stylized crosses or New Age crystals often pop up on fashion jewelry.[131] Critics often charge that Christmas has turned into a secular, materialistic occasion devoid of its original sacred significance. In the U.S.A. alone, the religious publishing and products (RPP) market brings in $6 billion per year.[132]

GRAB YOUR SLEDGEHAMMER

Your business may involve tourism, sports, design, music, or any one of many verticals that elevate certain people, objects, and places to sacred status. In our global consumer culture, "religious" observances definitely are not confined to church. Cult products like Apple, Nike, HGTV, Oprah, or for some even Kraft Mac and Cheese inspire slavish devotion.

One way to add an extra layer of value to what you sell is to enshrine it as part of a collection that is set apart from "ordinary" items. An item is sacralized as soon as it enters a collection, and it takes on special significance to the collector that outsiders may find hard to comprehend. For example, you may know someone who collects matchbooks that mark visits to out-of-town restaurants: Just try to use one of these books if you actually need to light a match. Consumers take their collections seriously, and you should, too.

Distribution and Retailing

Say goodbye to the wall between retailers and shoppers as well. Everyday folks are create their own online stores by the thousands, as *P2P (peer-to-peer) commerce* grows by leaps and bounds. Consumers manage their own inventories and trade with one another in staggering numbers. One reason for this boom is the emerging *P2P payments* industry, where platforms including PayPal, Venmo, Square and Zelle turn each of us into bankers.

eBay alone boasts over one billion live listings and 171 million active buyers.[133] Although eBay seems to have grown out of its homegrown "artisanal" character in its early days as many sellers adopt sophisticated marketing techniques, it's still a platform that allows anyone with used clothing (or memorabilia or just about anything else…), a shipping box, and a dream to become a retailer.

Direct Selling: Retailers vs. Customers

What do wine, sex toys, and plastic containers have in common? Hordes of housewives around the world sell all of them at *home parties*. In each case, women (primarily) are recruited to act as distributors on behalf of companies that represent a huge range of products and services. In some cases, they find the path to entrepreneurship when they go on to open their own businesses in partnership with a *direct selling* company. Make no mistake: The industry is a money machine. In 2016, these producers/consumers purchased about $35.54 billion in the U.S. alone, including over $12 billion just for wellness products.[134]

About 20.5 million people were involved in direct selling in the United States in 2016. The very large majority of distributors engage in direct selling part time – many are simply avid customers who decided to practice what they preach by becoming their own in-house (literally, in their own house) wholesalers, advertisers and sales force.

Roughly ¼ of those who start down this path go on to build independent businesses as direct sellers. This means they actively manage a customer base, and sponsor still other distributors they recruit for their network who share a portion of their commissions with them. In addition, a very high proportion of direct selling distributors purchase the products they sell to others for their own use as well (at a nice discount). The industry euphemistically refers to this practice as *internal consumption*.[135] It's yet another way that the wall between retailers and consumers is coming down.

The humble Tupperware party concept has morphed into a multibillion-dollar industry that turns housewives into sophisticated distributors.

Owning vs. Leasing

The *sharing economy* is one of the most disruptive forces we have ever witnessed in marketing. Whether they borrow a neighbor's bike, a power saw or a kitchen appliance, stay in a stranger's home, watch people's pets, give neighborhood tours, or bypass a taxi to grab a ride home with an Uber driver, everyday people relentlessly break down the wall between amateurs and professional service providers. According to one estimate, about ¼ of the U.S. population used a sharing economy service at least once in the past year.[136]

The trend toward pooling resources brings up a big question: Why buy when you can rent? Yet another wall that's tumbling down: We used to value objects we could own; whether nice clothes, power tools or record albums. The drive to acquire possessions underlies some of the basic tenets of capitalism. Taking title to a house or a car traditionally is a major milestone for many and a marker that a person has come of age.

Throw that ego trip out the window of your rented home. Today many consumers want to <u>avoid</u> ownership and the financial costs and responsibilities that come with it. For example, Americans lease rather than buy more new vehicles than ever; today this is the case in about 1/3 of transactions.[137] Cadillac recognized this trend, and the carmaker's answer is its "Book Cadillac" program that gives participants the ability to sample a range of cars because they can exchange their Cadillacs up to eighteen times per year.[138]

The sharing economy makes it easy to barter, trade and rent rather than own. We pay for cars by the hour, rent our neighbors' power tools, lease a "makerspace" to access 3D printers and other sophisticated equipment, and stream music rather than download it. This year about six million women "borrowed" gowns and other items from the apparel rental company Rent the Runway to the tune of over $100 million in revenue.[139] Even the number of teenagers who bother to obtain a driver's license is in decline: In a 2014 study, just 24.5 percent of 16-year-olds had a license, a 47 percent decrease from 1983. The top three reasons kids gave for foregoing this ritual were: "too busy or not enough time to get a driver's license" (37 percent), "owning and maintaining a vehicle is too expensive" (32 percent), and "able to get transportation from others" (31 percent).[140]

In the last year, about 796,000 people rented a Zipcar in the U.S.[141]

Pride of ownership recedes as our relationships with objects become more ephemeral. We would rather "rent" an experience than own a thing. The choice to rent a Zipcar for an hour or two rather than to invest in wheels to call your own is typical of this thinking. Given that it costs about $9,000 to own and maintain a car each year, paying in small increments on an on-demand basis makes a lot of sense for many of us, especially city dwellers.

GRAB YOUR SLEDGEHAMMER

Ironically, new tech platforms enable a return to old school bartering models, where people trade everything from power tools gathering dust in their garages to personal services like cleaning or minor repairs.

Can you create a new business model that facilitates this process? If you operate physical locations, do you have excess capacity you can rent to host "swap meets" that will create bonds with the local community?

Walls get in the way of sharing. They're coming down fast.

WALL #5:
Male vs. Female

A bestselling book once proclaimed, "men are from Mars, women are from Venus."[142] A tidy dichotomy, but unfortunately one that doesn't apply so well today (if it ever did).

The raging cultural war over who has the right to use a men's or women's bathroom testifies to the volatility of this category. Just what does it mean to be male, female, agender, cis, feminine-of-center, FtM, genderqueer, third gender, or any one of numerous terms that vie today to replace the man/woman dichotomy of old?[143]

There's no doubt that gender identity is a crucial component of a consumer's self-concept. People often conform to their culture's expectations about how those of their gender should act, dress, or speak; we refer to these sets of expectations as *sex roles*.

And there's little doubt that at least some of the stereotypes about gender differences in consumption are valid overall. Consider the gender differences market researchers observe when they compare the food preferences of men to those of women. Women eat more fruit; men are more likely to eat meat. As one food writer put it, "Boy food doesn't grow. It is hunted or killed."[144] Indeed, consumers tend to view meat as a masculine product. In one case a company that sells soy patties found that men viewed the food as feminine, so its solution was to add artificial grill marks on the patties to make them look like cuts of meat.[145]

Of course, advertisers themselves encourage these stereotypes. A study that tracked advertising in eight male magazines with primarily male readerships (ranging from *Maxim* to *Golf Digest*) reported that most contain many ads that can contribute to *hyper-masculinity* because of heavy emphasis on violence, dangerousness, and callous attitudes toward women and sex.[146]

To promote its Dr. Pepper Ten drink, the company sent a mobile "Man Cave" to U.S. cities. The trailer parked in "testosterone zones" such as ball fields or car shows, where it gave men a place to watch TV and play video games. The accompanying advertising campaign featured a muscled commando type who totes a space-age weapon. "Hey ladies, enjoying the film?" he asks. "'Course not. Because this is our movie, and Dr. Pepper Ten is our soda."[147]

On the other hand, it should not be news that sex roles (in a modern society at least) are always a work in progress. A behavior or product that's considered taboo for one gender or another today may come into vogue tomorrow. How about those skirt-wearing men we see in progressive cities like Seattle?

And, traditional depictions of sex roles that we accepted without a shrug a few years ago we may deem offensive today. A European ad for designer Dolce & Gabbana portrayed a group of sweaty men in tight jeans surrounding a woman wearing spike heels whom they've pinned to the ground. This aggressiveness did not go over so well among many contemporary consumers as it once might have -- when for example a husband in a 1960s coffee ad threatened to spank his wife if she didn't wise up and buy the right brand.

Advertising that emphasizes gratuitous sexual imagery is no longer "politically correct," but still common.

Androgyny: The Best of Both Worlds?

Androgyny refers to the possession of both masculine and feminine traits.[148] The growing prevalence (or at least visibility) of androgynous people obliterates the traditional gender dichotomy that has guided so many marketing strategies.

Adolescent males known as *wakashu* (like the one to the left of the geisha here), who were sexually available to both men and women, were regarded as the epitome of beauty in early modern Japan before the country adopted Western sexual mores in the late 1800s.[149]

As we might expect, this blurring of boundaries is more widely accepted in some cultures than in others. For example, although acceptance of homosexuality varies in Asian cultures, it doesn't occur to most Asians to assume that a man with feminine qualities is gay. A survey of Korean consumers found that more than 66 percent of men and 57 percent of women younger than age 40 were living self-described "androgynous" lifestyles. But the respondents didn't link those choices with sexual orientation. Although Koreans nickname males with feminine interests "flower men," they don't consider this to be a derogatory term.[150] In Japan, men called *gyaru-o* ("male gals") are common on city streets. Tanned and meticulously dressed (and usually heterosexual), these fops cruise Tokyo's stylish boutiques.[151]

Androgyny is all the rage in the fashion industry as well. One trend in menswear shows is to use both waifish male models and boyish female models to exhibit clothes that traditionally appear in womenswear collections. Gucci, Burberry, and Balenciaga dispensed with gender distinctions when these fashion houses combined their womenswear and menswear fashion shows. Balenciaga's creative director commented, "Gender doesn't exist anymore. Man or woman, we can choose what we want to be."[152] Some department stores devote floor space to unisex clothing. Selfridges in the U.K. recently launched the Agender Project—a section of the store showcases gender-spanning lines, such as Nicopanda, Comme des Garçons, and Gareth Pugh.[153]

Many pop culture icons are poster children for androgyny, such as Dr. Frank-N-Furter (originally portrayed by Tim Curry) in the *Rocky Horror Picture Show*, the celebrity drag queen Ru Paul, the comedian Eddie Izzard, Lady Gaga, the New York Dolls, the late Prince, and Annie Lennox.

GRAB YOUR SLEDGEHAMMER

Androgyny can open new markets if marketers have the courage to peek over the wall that separates genders. Some companies that sell exclusively to one gender, for example, may decide to test the waters with the other sex when they promote *gender-bending products*. This term refers to traditionally sex-typed items that a brand adapts to the opposite gender, such as the recent profusion of pink guns for women. Here are some other gender benders:[154]

- American Girl introduced its first boy doll. Logan Everett sports perfect hair, a hipster T-shirt and dark-wash jeans, and he plays the drums in a band.[155]

- Old Spice has long been known as the brand Dad keeps in his medicine cabinet, but young women who like the scent and the relatively low price are tuning into the deodorant as well. This resurgence is a bit ironic, because the first product the company introduced in 1937 was a women's fragrance.

- Febreze is an odor-neutralizing line of products that Procter & Gamble (P&G) markets to women for housecleaning. However, P&G finds that a lot of men spray it on their clothes to delay doing laundry. And in Vietnam, where the product is called Ambi Pur, men who ride motor scooters use it as a deodorizing spray for their helmets.[156]

- Startup companies like Older Brother sell unisex clothing, and MeUndies makes underwear for men and women including bright pink men's boxers and camo-print women's bikinis. Its founder explains, "Our women's boy short is essentially the men's boxer brief without the pouch, while our men's brief is essentially the women's bikini cut with a pouch."[157]

- More than three million British men say they wear makeup such as "manscara" and "guyliner." A third of these users borrow cosmetics from their wives or girlfriends, but the online retailer MMUK Man exclusively sells products for men.[158]

The End of Gender Binarism?

To put things in perspective, the *GLBTQ* (gay, lesbian, bisexual, transgender, and questioning) market is about as large as the Asian-American population (currently at about 12 million people). These consumers spend in the range of $250 billion to $350 billion a year. A Simmons study of readers of gay publications found that these readers are almost 12 times more likely to hold professional jobs, twice as likely to own a vacation home, and eight times more likely to own a notebook computer compared to heterosexuals.[159]

Of late the cultural spotlight has turned on the "T" in this acronym. Transgender people suddenly are much more visible. No doubt this new prominence has been helped along by the media attention paid to a character in the popular TV show *Orange is the New Black*, and certainly by the debut of former athlete and reality TV star Bruce Jenner in her new identity as Caitlin Jenner on the cover of *Vogue*.

Our definitions of gender continue to evolve as a global *third-gender movement* picks up steam:

- Australia's High Court recently ruled that a person there was allowed to register gender as "nonspecific" on official documents.

- Nepal issues citizenship papers with a "third gender" category.

- Germany allows parents of *intersex children* — those born with both genitals, or ambiguous sex characteristics — to mark their birth certificates with an X.[160]

- California allows residents to declare a "third gender" on their drivers' licenses.[161]

- In 2014, Facebook began to allow users to choose among 58 defined genders—along with a write-in option — that ranged from "gender fluid" to "intersex" and simply "neither."[162] Other social networks followed suit, as did some dating apps.

- In 2015, the University of California joined colleges around the country when it added "gender nonconforming" and "genderqueer" to its applications alongside transgender, male, and female.

United Colors of Benetton caused a stir when a recent ad campaign featured Lea T, a transgender Brazilian model.[163]

Thus it seems that *gender binarism* -- the classification of gender into two distinct, opposite and disconnected forms of masculine and feminine is giving way to *gender benders*, or people who "bend" traditional sex roles.[164]

Most social scientists have always viewed sexuality as a continuum rather than a dichotomy. Masculinity and femininity are social constructions that vary across cultures and historical periods. However, in Western culture we seem to have reached a watershed moment when people question even the anchor points of this continuum. The wall that separates men and women has never been more fragile.

We can expect to see gender-neutral icons like this one popping up on public restrooms and other locations as the third-gender movement picks up steam.

WALL #6:
Work vs. Play

At the turn of the millennium, the U.S. military was having a hard time convincing young men to enlist for "adventures" in Iraq and elsewhere. One solution: Turn war into an exciting videogame. *America's Army* allowed potential recruits to experience the heat of battle from the comfort of a gaming console. Although most details are quite accurate, the game conveniently omits any sound effects or gory stuff when a solider gets killed. Players learn that war is fun.[165]

We used to draw a line between work and play. No longer. Today employees expect to respond to company emails on weekends. In turn they devote big chunks of the workday to shopping or playing online games -- over 1/3 of American workers admit to browsing for goodies online while on company time.[166] For an increasing number of workers, *telecommuting* dissolves the wall that separates home vs. office. In 2016, a Gallup Poll reported that 43% of U.S. employees say they spend at least some time working from home.[167]

We see the work versus play wall crumbling when we look at what people wear to work or play: Today "work clothes" in some industries consist of jeans and t-shirts (maybe even flip flops on Casual Fridays), while menswear designers offer modified suits to wear during off-hours (some with cut-off sleeves or other modifications).[168]

Work Becomes Play

A few years ago a Gallup survey revealed a sobering statistic: Over 70% of U.S. workers reported they were "not engaged" or "actively disengaged" with their jobs.[169] By one estimate, employee disengagement costs the U.S economy 350 billion dollars per year in lost productivity, accidents, theft and turnover.[170]

At least some forward-thinking organizations are fighting back. Although job prospects may not be bright for everyone in today's economy, knowledge workers with attractive skills often can pick and choose among corporate suitors. In many cases, these choices revolve less around salary and benefits, and more around which workplace offers the most amenities to make going to the office almost seem like a trip to a country club.

Perks like free food, game rooms, and sometimes even beer kegs in the break room beckon. Yelp offers an on-site minibar. Abercrombie & Fitch gives employees perky little scooters to travel around the office in style. Charles Schwab offers chair massages. During a visit to Zappos' HQ in Las Vegas, I witnessed call center workers participating in fun activities that "spontaneously" happened at various points during the work day, such as a contest to see who could drop an egg without breaking it from a third story atrium.[171] New Age employee retention strategies turn work into play.

Clearly, many more companies need to take steps to wake up their workforces. The same goes for disengaged students (welcome to my world), and disengaged customers. While traditional ROI (Return on Investment) is a key metric today, another kind of *ROI (Return on Involvement)* may be equally as important – but often overlooked.

Gamification: This is NOT a Game!

Gamification strategies turn work into play, as we compete to win points and badges when we complete mundane tasks.

The pressure to build engagement explains why gamification strategies have become attractive to so many managers, marketers, and even to some crusty old professors. No, this doesn't mean playing Candy Crush at your desk. These approaches involve the application of gaming elements to non-game contexts. Turning work into play is huge these days: A Boston Retail Partners 2017 survey reported that almost nine out of 10 retailers expect to adopt gamification methods in the next five years.[172]

In fact, games do offer many elements that can increase engagement. That's why games of Monopoly, poker, Halo or even Chutes & Ladders for the younger set (and their patient grandparents) can go on seemingly forever. The ultimate goal is that players enter a *flow state* where they become totally immersed in the experience. Ideally they lose track of time as they focus exclusively on the game (casinos encourage this mindlessness when they conveniently make sure there are no clocks on the walls).

Most gamification applications don't go quite so far, but even some attempt to make mundane or boring tasks "fun" is better than accepting the *status quo*. For example, Microsoft in India devised an ingenious solution to motivate employees who had to spend tedious hours combing through computer code to spot errors: The company turned the chore into a competition.[173]

Gaming elements that organizations can import include:

- Learning or problem solving
- A balance of structure and exploration
- Multiple short and long term goals
- Rapid and frequent feedback
- A reward for most or all efforts in the form of a badge or a virtual product
- Friendly competition in a low-risk environment

Play Becomes Work

From the Silk Road online market for illegal drugs, to the sexual harassment of female gamers, to illicit sites that share child pornography, to cyberbullying, the Internet surely has a very dark side. Add exploited workers to the list: The videogame industry has long been troubled by the widespread practice of *gold farming*. This term refers to the practice of paying minimal wages to primarily Chinese workers who play games for 12 monotonous hours per day in order to rack up virtual currency that their employers trade for cash.[174] Surely, that's play become work.

Regimented Kids and Helicopter Parents

Chinese videogamers-for-hire aren't the only ones who seem to have erased the boundary between work and play. The concept of "free play" that most of us grew up with seems to be in short supply these days. It's hard work to be a kid!

Helicopter parents engage in the practice of over-parenting. They're obsessed with their children's activities and love to micro-manage almost every second of the day. If it won't look good on the 'ol college resume, then bag it. As one critic of this overscheduled lifestyle lamented:

Kids no longer go outside and hit the baseball. They have a game. They no longer sit and color, they go to art class. There is no doubt that they are spending their time in constructive activities that provide them with fun and useful skills. But they are spending a lot time in these activities and everything is so structured that everybody is stressed.[175]

Note: I even see this at the college level. It's only in the past few years that I've gotten calls from parents who are trying to work out their child's schedule for them or who want to dispute a grade I've assigned. In most cases the student isn't even involved in the discussion!

The Quantified Self

An entrepreneur named Dave Asprey is making a fortune with "Bulletproof Coffee," a blend of caffeine, butter and medium-chain triglyceride oil derived from coconut oil that supposedly increases energy and imparts cognitive clarity. Asprey's podcast called *Bulletproof Radio*, where he describes the formula's effects, has been downloaded well over 10 million times.[176]

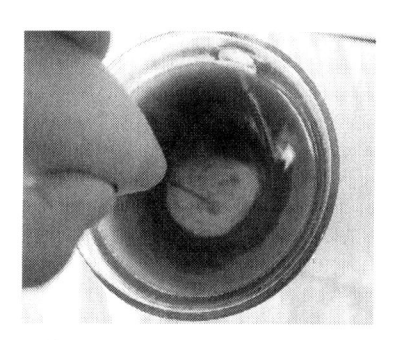

Bulletproof Coffee blends a hefty dose of butter with other ingredients to supposedly create a wonder drink.

Biohackers come in all shapes and sizes. Some like Asprey drink coffee laced with fat. Some wear a headband that electrically stimulates the brain to improve cognition. Others meticulously track and record everything they eat, and dabble in supplements that purport to improve mental and physical performance. A few hardy souls even have a light-up implant surgically inserted into their arms to monitor biometric data that changes color when levels are abnormal.

Biohackers zealously harness data to self-regulate. They share a belief that individuals have the power to enlist biotechnology in the service of enhanced mental and physical well-being. Simply put, these "enthusiasts" aim to build an improved human being. As one *transhumanist* stated, "I can't really rely on my brain, but I can rely on the data my body produces." [177]

These geeks take the practice of obtaining feedback from their bodies to an extreme, but the rest of us also monitor ourselves like never before. Apps turn play into work, as we zealously track our progress at dieting, exercise and also compulsively share our opinions (solicited or not) about restaurants, hotels, and even dating partners. We obsess about food intake, calories burned, the impact of the light from phone screens on sleep patterns, or even the money we spend on indulgences when we deviate from our health regimens.

And, we eagerly grab the latest devices to aid us in our quest to quantify: Smartphones with pedometers, smart watches, Fitbit bands, and even GPS devices that monitor gait to detect early onset of Alzheimer's. New devices appear almost daily: A contact lens that measures blood sugar in a diabetic's tears. A football helmet that tracks the severity of blows to the head. A sensor that reports when a resident in a nursing home has taken a fall.

GRAB YOUR SLEDGEHAMMER

A thriving industry caters to our yearning to self-quantify. Numerous startups are betting that consumers will outsource their self-regulation in the hope of becoming better, brighter, augmented versions of themselves. Companies hawk apps and other devices that measure how much we sleep, eat, walk, and spend.

Some of these hi-tech tools are socially grounded; their success hinges upon consumers' willingness to share their data with their networks to obtain reinforcement, feedback – and sometimes a modicum of shame that drives them to do better. As a consequence, these "wellness" platforms create pools of big data, which rightly or wrongly, are available for companies to track our most bio-basic behaviors.

The goal of self-improvement through knowledge has been around at least since the ancient Greeks, who prized *physical culture* as well as the intellect. The first recorded instance of a person who sought gain understanding through self-tracking is Sanctorius of Padua, who in the 16th century recorded his own weight versus food intake and waste over a 30 year period, to understand energy expenditures in living systems (he needed to get out more!).[178] The Italian Renaissance later sparked renewed interest in the perfection of the body. The first U.S. gymnasium opened in 1823, and John Harvey Kellogg's famous sanitarium in Battle Creek, Michigan attracted thousands of affluent guests (Kellogg's' line of "healthy" cereals became a foundation of the natural food industry).[179]

Still, for most of human history people rarely quantified their behaviors to guide their personal lives (with the exception of personal finances and sports betting, perhaps). Most likely, the regime of recordkeeping of such seemingly trivial things as our pastimes and moods in the pre-digitized world seemed not only burdensome, but also somewhat unnecessary and vaguely narcissistic. Individuals on the whole were happy to adopt the naturalist belief that the human being is able to optimize his or her activities based upon intuition and memory.

The wearable tech industry is exploding, largely due to our desire to self-regulate our physical activity – and thus to work at play.

Today in contrast we each live in a digital fishbowl, with access to a huge amount of biometric information, and the technology to share it. Thus for many the urge to not only record but also to compare our own "normal" to other peoples' "normal" is irresistible and unrelenting. Unlike the physical culture enthusiasts of earlier eras, now we are able to digitally track and fastidiously record most facets of our analogue and digital lives – from sleep patterns to nutrition, health, location and social interactions. This practice even has a name: *Lifelogging*.[180]

To See and Be Seen

Our daily lives offer a multitude of opportunities and pressures for individuals to share content, and thus to "be seen" by others online. When you are alone your behaviors may be uninhibited – you might not bother to shave, or inhale a bag of candy bars. However, the possibility of being seen (albeit digitally) encourages people to self-regulate their behavior. They look to technology to help them live up to social expectations. Platforms such as Map My Fitness and Nike + GPS allow users to post updates on their fitness regimens in order to receive encouraging feedback from members of their networks.

Others seem to doubt their own abilities to self-regulate, to the extent that they actually choose to submit to *public shaming* to keep them on track toward their goals. There is an increasing trend to use this tactic in self-regulation, whereby apps provide negative reinforcement to make users achieve their goals. Gym Pact pays cash rewards if users meet their fitness goals – but applies financial penalties if they don't. Aherk employs social penalties instead: When users don't meet their goal, the site poses embarrassing photos of them (previously supplied when they signed up for the service) to their network! These types of applications mean that we are delegating agency to our devices even when they deliver negative reinforcement to us in thanks for our acquiescence.

Folks, this "play" really is hard work.

WALL #7:
Body vs. Belongings

Members of every culture adorn their bodies with artifacts like clothing and jewelry, and change these out to suit their moods or social demands. But today, we don't just put things <u>on</u>; we put things <u>in</u>. Permanent tattoos, breast, lip, buttock and cheek implants, artificial hips, knees and prostheses, pacemakers, and embedded computer chips obliterate the traditional boundary between what we're born with and what we own. The body is morphing into a product delivery platform. In a very real sense, we are what we own and we own what we are. The wall between our physical bodies and our possessions has never been more tenuous.

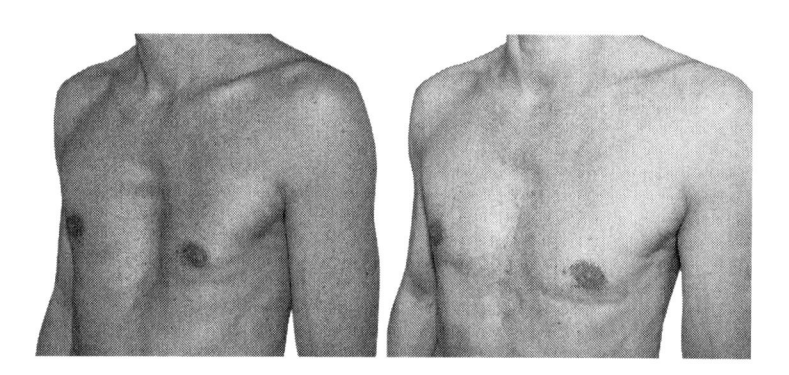

We don't just put things <u>on</u>; we put things <u>in</u>. Pectoral implants have joined breast enhancements and other forms of plastic surgery as commonplace procedures for consumers who want to modify their bodies.

You Are What You Buy

Way back in 1890, the pioneering psychologist William James wrote, "*A man's self is the sum total of all that he can call his.*"[181] And that was before iPhones, Diesel jeans, and hoverboards!

When researchers asked children of various ages to create "who am I?" collages, for which they chose pictures that represented their selves, older kids between middle childhood and early adolescence were more likely to insert photos of branded merchandise. Also, as they aged, their feelings about these objects evolved from concrete relationships (e.g., "I own it") to more sophisticated, abstract relationships (e.g., "It is like me").[182]

We are *attached* to an object when we rely on it to maintain our self-concept.[183] Objects act as a security blanket when they reinforce our identities, especially in unfamiliar situations. For example, students who decorate their dorm rooms with personal items are less likely to drop out of college. This coping process may protect the self from being diluted in a strange environment.[184]

Self-image congruence models suggest that we choose products when their attributes match some aspect of the self.[185] And, when we choose a product that we think is aesthetically pleasing, this choice makes us feel better about ourselves.[186] Indeed recent research that included brain wave measures such as *functional magnetic resonance imaging (fMRI)* showed that when a person has a close relationship with a brand this activates the insula, a brain area responsible for urging, addiction, loss aversion, and interpersonal love.[187]

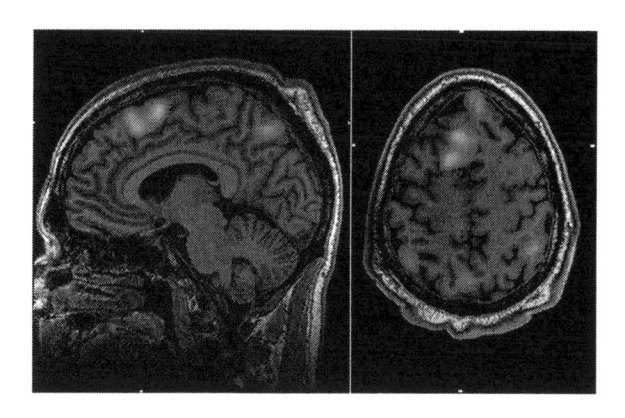

Neuromarketing techniques show how pleasure centers in our brains light up when we think about our favorite brands.

These emotional connections make people defensive of their favorite brands if they come across negative information about them. A comment by a respondent (a 32-year-old male) in one study nicely illustrates this bond: *"My BMW is my wingman, my twin. I would never diss it for another car because that would be like dissing my twin brother or worse, dissing myself."*[188]

This guy's fondness for his vehicle is hardly unique; more than a third of Americans have nicknames for their cars. That bond explains the wording of a recent TV commercial for SafeAuto insurance as a Mom drives her kids around in a well-used minivan: "For years you and this supercharged piece of eye candy have done much more than make car payments, buy gas and change the oil. You've lived, really lived, and you're most certainly not done..."[189]

Congruence models assume a process of *cognitive matching* between a product's attributes and the consumer's self-image.[190] Over time we tend to form relationships with products that resemble the bonds we create with other people: These include love, unrequited love (we yearn for it but can't have it), respect, and perhaps even fear or hate ("why is my computer out to get me?").[191] Studies even report that after a "breakup" with a brand, people tend to develop strong negative feelings and will go to great lengths to discredit the item, including bad-mouthing and even vandalism.[192]

Research largely supports the idea of congruence between product usage and self-image. One of the earliest studies to examine this process found that car owners' ratings of themselves tended to match their perceptions of their cars: Pontiac drivers saw themselves as more active and flashy than did Volkswagen drivers.[193] Indeed, a German study found that observers were able to match photos of male and female drivers to pictures of the cars they drove almost 70 percent of the time.[194] Researchers also report congruity between consumers and their most preferred brands of beer, soap, toothpaste, and cigarettes relative to their least preferred brands, as well as between consumers' self-images and their favorite stores.[195]

The Body as Billboard

The body truly has become a blank canvas for people to alter at will. Technology removes much of the risk from momentous decisions we used to fret over: "Should I change my hair color?" "How will I look in those expensive glasses?" "Do those jeans make me look fat?" True, these questions are not exactly on the same scale as "How do I bring about world peace?," but they certainly cause a lot of anguish for many of us.

But rest easy, because help is here. Today a plethora of websites like dailymakeover.com and myvirtualmodel.com offer a risk-free way to modify your hair, makeup, glasses, and even physical dimensions like bust size.

GRAB YOUR SLEDGEHAMMER

The calculus of *perceived risk* -- will this product hurt me, bankrupt me, embarrass me? -- is one of the most important considerations of any purchase, Therefore, shortcuts that allow a buyer to view the outcome before committing to it potentially will transform the decision-making landscape for many products and services beyond hairstyles or tight blue jeans.

Think about the potential for home furnishings, plastic surgery, customized car design, and virtually any other purchase that requires a leap of faith today. Embrace technologies that allow your customers to reduce perceived risk, and you knock down a huge barrier to purchase.

Identity marketing is a promotional strategy that encourages consumers to alter some part of their bodies to advertise for a branded product. Air New Zealand created "cranial billboards" in exchange for a round-trip ticket to New Zealand—30 Los Angeles participants shaved their heads and walked around with an ad for the airline on their skulls.[196]

Temporary tattoos of brand logos are common these days (along with a fair amount of permanent ones).[197] Companies hand them out like candy at sporting events, concerts and other public venues. This idea is hardly new; bubble gum companies in the 19th century distributed crudely made versions of today's temporary tats, and then in 1890 Cracker Jack included them as one of their "prize in every box" promotions.[198]

But today the stakes are bigger: Reebok recently set up a pop-up tattoo shop at an event in Sweden and gave away thousands of dollars in prizes to the fan who got the biggest version of the brands' new triangle logo (not a temporary one). The lucky winner's right thigh is, shall we say, Reebok's for life.[199]

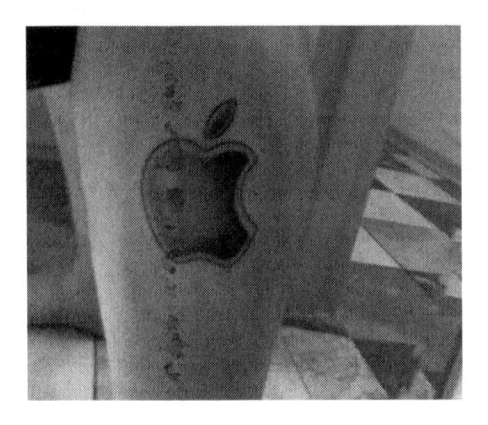

Brand logo tattoos (temporary or permanent) bond the self with possessions.

The Extended Self: You Are What You Buy

Our fixations with products go way beyond the occasional tattoo. Some of us willingly (and perhaps eagerly) label ourselves as fanatics about a cherished product.[200] Consider shoes, for example: You don't have to be Carrie of *Sex and the City* fame to acknowledge that many people feel a strong bond to their footwear. The singer Mariah Carey recently posted a photo of her huge shoe closet on Instagram and labeled it, "Always my favorite room in the house... #shoes #shoes #moreshoes."[201]

One study found that people commonly view their shoes as magical emblems of the self; Cinderella-like vehicles for self-transformation. A common theme that emerged was that a pair of shoes the person obtained when younger—whether a first pair of leather shoes, a first pair of high heels, or a first pair of cowboy boots—had a big impact even later in life. These experiences were similar to those we see in such well-known fairy tales and stories as Dorothy's red shoes in *The Wizard of Oz*, Karen's magical red shoes in Hans Christian Anderson's *The Red Shoes*, and Cinderella's glass slippers.[202]

Some consumers view their favorite shoes as a vehicle of transformation.

In addition to shoes, of course, many material objects—ranging from personal possessions and pets to national monuments or landmarks—help to form a person's identity. Just about everyone can name a valued possession that has a lot of the self "wrapped up" in it, whether it is a beloved photograph, a trophy, an old shirt, a car, or a cat. Indeed, usually we can construct a pretty accurate "biography" of someone when we simply catalog the items he displays in his bedroom or office.

A study illustrates that the product's relationship to the owner doesn't even have to be that strong to influence a consumer's self-concept. In one experiment, researchers approached women in a shopping mall and gave them one of two shopping bags to walk around with for an hour. Women who received a bag from Victoria's Secret later reported to the researchers that they felt more sensual and glamorous than those who were given a more mundane bag. In another experiment, MBA students were asked to take notes for 6 weeks using a pen embossed with the MIT logo; they reported feeling smarter at the end of the term.[203]

Those external objects that we consider a part of us constitute the *extended self*. In some cultures, people literally incorporate objects into the self: They lick new possessions, take the names of conquered enemies (or in some cases eat them), or bury the dead with their possessions.[204]

We continue to discover new ways to integrate man-made products into our physical bodies. The use of foreign materials to replace or supplement human body parts is not necessarily new (remember George

Washington's infamous wooden teeth), but recent advances in technology continue to erode the barrier between self and not-self:[205]

- According to the American Society for Aesthetic Plastic Surgery, Americans get more than nine million cosmetic surgical and non-surgical procedures in a year. The most frequently performed surgical procedure is breast augmentation, which typically involves the integration of man-made silicon implants with the patient's organic material.

- More than four million Americans have an artificial knee.

- At least prior to his arrest for murder that made global headlines, the South African track star Oscar Pistorious competed against world-class runners with two artificial legs made of carbon – his nickname was "Blade Runner." Nike teamed with orthopedics company Össur to introduce its first sprinting prosthesis, called the Nike Sole, perhaps the first commercially scalable transformation of disabled athletes into "superabled" athletes.

- More than 200,000 people now have cochlear implants that deliver sound from a microphone directly to the auditory nerve. Other neural implants recognize when epileptic seizures are about to occur and stimulate the brain to stop them. A paraplegic woman who wore a motorized exoskeleton walked the route of the London Marathon over a period of 17 days.

Researchers describe four levels of the extended self, ranging from personal objects to places and things that allow people to feel as though they are rooted in their larger social environments:[206]

1. *Individual level.* Consumers include many of their personal possessions in self-definition. These products can include jewelry,

cars, clothing, and so on. The saying, "You are what you wear," reflects the belief that one's things are a part of one's identity.

2. *Family level.* This part of the extended self includes a consumer's residence and the furnishings in it. We can think of the house as a symbolic body for the family, and the place where we live often is a central aspect of who we are. In addition, our children often reflect upon our self-worth; a big driver for parents to splurge on fancy clothing, tutors, and even etiquette classes for their little darlings.

3. *Community level.* It is common for consumers to describe themselves in terms of the neighborhood or town from which they come. For farm families or other residents with close ties to a community, this sense of belonging is particularly important. "I'm from Brooklyn. Fuggedaboutit!"

4. *Group level.* We regard our attachments to key social groups as a part of the self. These links are responsible for big chunks of our identities, whether they're based upon political affiliation, religion, athletic teams, or perhaps a love for one's *alma mater*.

GRAB YOUR SLEDGEHAMMER

There's no doubt about it: We buy a huge range of products because of a drive to enhance the extended self. Athletic wear merchandisers get this, but companies in other verticals may not. Brands that link the consumer to key elements of the self, whether these are schools, favorite musical artists, old neighborhoods, or coveted identities like "successful executive" or "glam girl" have a leg up over others that don't such a good job connecting to the extended self-concept.

You Buy What You Are

We're especially likely to rely upon consumption information to define the self when we have yet to completely form a social identity. This typically happens when we have to play a new role in life. Think, for example, of the insecurity many people feel when they start college, or reenter the dating market after exiting a long-term relationship. *Symbolic self-completion theory* proposes that people who have an incomplete self-definition tend to complete this identity when they acquire and display symbols they associate with that role.[207]

A study of MBA students carefully chronicled the markers of "executive success" that these managers-in-training displayed, such as luxury watches, fancy briefcases, and the like. Sure enough, the researchers found that those students who scored lower on measures of actual achievement (GPA, number of interviews, etc.) were more likely to sport these products.

In another study that hits a bit closer to home, less-accomplished professors (in terms of number of publications, etc.) were more likely to hang a large number of diplomas, certifications, and other badges of scholarly achievement on their office walls.[208] This compensatory process is important, because it implies that it's novices rather than experts who are more likely to acquire products that are stereotypically linked to a role.

Some years ago – back in the day when it was still something of a news story that sizeable numbers of young women were flooding into management roles -- I conducted several studies when I was on the faculty at New York University to explore how role insecurity related to choices of "appropriate professional apparel." I was motivated by the anxiety my female MBA students expressed to me about whether the clothing they wore to work would send the appropriate signals. At that time, most of them chose the safe route (there's that notion of "perceived risk" rearing its ugly head again). They dressed as male clones in very severe, dark suits – but they weren't happy about it because they felt they had to sacrifice their femininity in order to succeed in a man's world. This tension perseveres today, especially in the wake of the sexual harassment scandals we encounter in fields from politics and business to entertainment and the arts.

My research revealed an interesting anomaly: Although in most contexts we expect younger people to be the fashion trendsetters, in a business context the opposite was true. Using a sample of over 50,000 readers of a female executive magazine, we found instead that older, more experienced women were more likely to endorse a wide range of styles they felt were appropriate to wear to work. Like the anxious women I saw in my Manhattan classroom, the newbies were much more likely to believe that only a very constricted set of styles (essentially female versions of the male banker's suit) were OK.[209]

Younger, less-experienced women are more likely to rely upon external cues such as professional clothing to guide self-definition.

GRAB YOUR SLEDGEHAMMER

This finding and others like it leads to a somewhat paradoxical but important bit of strategic guidance: Whether in sports, business, design, other industries, it's the <u>beginners</u> who often are the best customers for products and services that conform to rigid standards.

If you sell sports equipment, career apparel, home furnishings, or any other type of product that links to roles consumers have to learn, it's fine to use accomplished experts as role models and endorsers. However, it's likely that your best customers are <u>not</u> experts, but rather people who are doing their best to learn the ropes.

"Clothes (and Other Stuff) Make the (Wo)Man"

So it seems that my female students and their sisters rely upon the signals they glean from their clothing to define their professional role. More generally, to what extent do the products we buy influence how we define ourselves? Social scientists who study relationships between thoughts and behaviors increasingly turn to the theory of *embodied cognition* for answers. A simple way to explain this perspective is that "states of the body modify states of the mind."[210] In other words, our behaviors and observations of what we do and buy shape our thoughts, <u>rather than vice versa</u>.

One of the most powerful illustrations of embodied cognition is the notion that our *body language* actually changes how we see ourselves. In one of the most widely viewed TED talks ever, a social psychologist discusses how *power posing* (standing in a confident way even if you don't feel confident) affects brain activity. Facebook COO Sheryl Sandberg's campaign to encourage women to "lean in" conveys the same idea.[211] This research is highly controversial, but it at least hints at the idea that <u>what we do influences what we feel</u>, rather than vice versa.

The embodied cognition approach is consistent with consumer behavior research that demonstrates how changes in self-concept can arise from usage of brands that convey different meanings. Indeed a pair of researchers used the term *enclothed cognition* in their work that showed how the symbolic meaning of clothing changes how people behave. In one study they asked respondents to wear a lab coat, which people associate with attentiveness and precise work. They found that subjects who wore the lab coat displayed enhanced performance on tasks that required them to pay close attention. But they also introduced a twist: When respondents were told the garment was in fact a painter's coat rather than a doctor's lab coat, the effects went away. In other words, the respondents interpreted the symbolic meaning of the clothing and then altered their behavior accordingly.[212]

It's tempting to point out that a study your humble author conducted more than 30 years ago on the "dress for success" phenomenon found similar results for students in job interview settings. In perhaps the best Ph.D. dissertation ever written (at least in your author's opinion), male candidates who wore professional attire acted more assertively and confidently during the interviews, and on average even asked for higher starting salaries![213]

This Wall is Down! What's Next?

As AI (artificial intelligence) tech advances, many of us are thinking a lot more about a fundamental question that sci-fi writers have grappled with for decades: What makes us human – and what separates a person from a machine? Way back in 1942, Isaac Asimov used a short story to introduce his classic *Laws of Robotics*:

1. A robot may not injure a human being or, through inaction, allow a human being to come to harm.

2. A robot must obey the orders given to it by human beings, except where such orders would conflict with the First Law.

3. A robot must protect its own existence as long as such protection does not conflict with the First or Second Law.[III]

Today, the question of what makes us human is much less theoretical. Self-driving cars threaten to replace truck drivers. IBM's Watson beats chess masters and veteran *Jeopardy* game show contestants. Movies and TV shows like *Blade Runner*, *Westworld*, and *Humans* that focus on the civil rights of synths, replicants and androids are center stage in popular culture. Alexa and Siri are our new guardian angels. Where does the person stop and the machine start?

The fusion between the physical body and technology leads some analysts to compare the modern consumer to a *cyborg*.[214] For sci-fi buffs, this term evokes the Cylons in the TV series *Battlestar Galactica*. More generally it refers to a person who lives a technologically enhanced existence, and who often possesses special abilities because s/he is linked to other parts of a larger system (like the Internet, perhaps).

So, where could the merger of body and tech lead us? In the short term, perhaps prurient interests will lead the way. Already several companies are working on *sexbots* that combine the physical realism of silicon dolls with the AI functionality that (ostensibly) allows the user to maintain an actual relationship with his or her special android.

The Harmony app (not to be confused with the eHarmony dating site, I assume) allows the user to customize an avatar for intimate conversations.[215] But that's only the beginning: The Realbotix company, which makes Realdoll silicon sex toys, makes this claim: "…the obvious next step in Realdoll evolution is integrating movement with the addition of robotic components…. the first animatronic Realdoll head, feature [es] neck articulation and facial expression, moving eyes, and the ability to lip sync with

---

[III] He later introduced a fourth or zeroth law that outranked the others: A robot may not harm humanity, or, by inaction, allow humanity to come to harm.

spoken audio."[216] Presumably the human and the bot will enjoy an e-cigarette afterwards.

Never fear, virtual sex is here...

For the longer term (and the more cerebral among us), we have the *Singularity movement*, which Ray Kurzweil (a prominent proponent) describes as "... a future period during which the pace of technological change will be so rapid, its impact so deep, that human life will be irreversibly transformed. Although neither utopian nor dystopian, this epoch will transform the concepts that we rely on to give meaning to our lives, from our business models to the cycle of human life, including death itself."[217]

Adherents of The Singularity believe that we are headed toward a new era, where human intelligence will merge with computer intelligence to create a man/machine hybrid civilization. They predict that the wall separating *Humans vs. Computers* will fall, perhaps even in our lifetimes.

We're far from there now, but it's hard to ignore the steady advance of work on the *Internet of Things (IoT)*. The IoT looks to be a tidal wave that will soon wash over many industry verticals. A person with a heart monitor implant, a farm animal with a biochip transponder, a smart thermostat that adjusts the temperature in a home and even raises and lowers the blinds to maintain equilibrium, or an automobile that has built-in sensors to alert the driver when tire pressure is low. All are plugged into the growing IoT.[218] It's all coming, and coming soon.

And thus, we steadily merge with the Internet of Things. The wall between body and possessions already is low. Soon it may be history.

AFTERWORD:
Then vs. Now

Our country is embroiled in a heated debate about walls: Whether and where to build one, how big it will be, who will pay for it. I hope I've made the case for <u>tearing down</u> walls instead – at least within the context of marketing strategy and consumer behavior. Walls are very comforting, because they assure us that we know where to put stuff and where to avoid treading. As they say, "good fences make good neighbors." If only we didn't live in such "interesting times," and we could afford this luxury!

Well, for the most part we don't. In this book, I've outlined seven basic, crucial, indispensable categories in consumer behavior, as well as numerous others that are part and parcel of our seemingly inexorable tendency to put things – and consumers – behind walls. Hopefully I've convinced you that these no longer exist, or at least are on life support. Like it or not, these walls are history.

The disappearance of these comforting dichotomies can dismay the traditionalist. But at the same time these changes can excite the visionary who embraces the freedom to redefine staid categories and create new hybrid products and services. Force yourself out of the box – move beyond outmoded classifications like male/female, work/play, and consumer/producer. Without a wall in front of you, you can sure see a lot farther.

But wait – it's not like there are <u>no</u> walls left. The sad truth – and perhaps the exception that proves the rule – is that some walls are stronger than ever. Here are two:

Rich Vs. Poor

Take a moment to ponder this: The 80 richest people in the world are worth $1.9 trillion. This is about the same amount shared by the 3.5 billion people who fall into the bottom half of the world's income.[219] And, the most affluent one percent of people worldwide control more than half the globe's total wealth.[220]

In the last few years the label *One Percenter* entered our nation's vocabulary. Beginning with the Occupy Wall Street movement where protestors camped out in cities across the United States, the spotlight has been on the people who earn the top one percent of income in our country. The wealthiest 160,000 U.S. families have as much wealth as the poorest 145 million families.[221]

The rising wall between rich and poor threatens to engulf our democracy.

Today one of the most pressing issues we hear about is *income inequality*; the extent to which resources are distributed unevenly within a population. Some critics believe this is the single biggest threat to our democracy (unfortunately, I can think of a few others as well).

One consequence of rising inequality is that more consumers worry about "falling behind" if a breadwinner loses his or her job, or if the family can no longer afford the cost of housing, transportation, and other necessities. For example, a researcher who conducted an in-depth study of residents of a rural trailer park identified one segment of consumers she called the *Reluctant Emigrants*. These people once lived in fixed-site homes but various economic problems forced them to move to the more affordable trailer park. Because their lives are on a downward trajectory, their primary concerns focus on security and protection.[222]

Citigroup strategists coined the term *plutonomy* to describe an economy that's driven by a fairly small number of rich people.[223] This term seems increasingly appropriate to describe the United States. The share of households in the middle-income bracket (earning $35,000 to $100,000 per year) is shrinking steadily.[224]

One indicator of income inequality is the *CEO pay ratio*, which benchmarks the salary of a company's chief executive to the earnings of a typical employee. That ratio grew from 20 in 1965 to 295.9 in 2013.[225] This gap is larger than most other countries. Recent reports indicate that the United States has the largest income inequality among developed countries. The only countries with a bigger disparity are Chile, Mexico, and Turkey.[226]

Social mobility refers to the "passage of individuals from one social class to another."[227] *Horizontal mobility* occurs when a person moves from one position to another that's roughly equivalent in social status; for instance, a nurse becomes an elementary school teacher. *Downward mobility* is, of course, movement none of us wants: Unfortunately we observe this pattern fairly often, as farmers and other displaced workers go on welfare rolls or join the ranks of the homeless. By one estimate, between 2.3 million and 3.5 million Americans experience homelessness in a year's time.[228]

Despite the well-deserved reputation of the United States as the "land of opportunity," social mobility today is a harder climb in the United States than in many other developed economies such as Canada, Denmark, Australia, Norway, Finland, Sweden, Germany, and Spain. One widely cited report, for example, found that the economic advantage of having an affluent father is much more likely to influence the fortune of his son in the United States than in most other Western countries.[229] Another analysis found that the likelihood of staying in the *same* social class as your parents is 0.47 in the United States, compared to only 0.15 in Denmark.[230]

The wall between rich and poor is actually getting higher rather than lower.

Right Vs. Left

Most of us know of families (perhaps our own) that have splintered due to acrimony about differences in political views today. It's a tough slog for many to even stay in the same room during Thanksgiving dinner.

The respected Pew Research Center recently documented these divisions in a large-scale survey. The Center reports:

> The divisions between Republicans and Democrats on fundamental political values – on government, race, immigration, national security, environmental protection and other areas – reached record levels during Barack Obama's presidency. In Donald Trump's first year as president, these gaps have grown even larger. And the magnitude of these differences dwarfs other divisions in society, along such lines as gender, race and ethnicity, religious observance or education.... In nearly every domain, across most of the roughly two dozen values questions tracked, views of Republicans and Republican-leaning independents and those of Democrats and Democratic leaners are now further apart than in the past... Currently, 44% of Democrats and Democratic leaners have a very unfavorable opinion of the GOP, based on yearly averages of Pew Research Center surveys; 45% of Republicans and Republican leaners view the Democratic Party very unfavorably.

In 1994, fewer than 20% in both parties viewed the opposing party very unfavorably.[231]

Clearly there are more walls to demolish.

ENDNOTES

1. https://hbr.org/2004/07/marketing-myopia, accessed November 26, 2017.

2. Trefis Team, "The Athleisure Trend Is Here To Stay," *Forbes* (October 6, 2016), https://www.forbes.com/sites/greatspeculations/2016/10/06/the-athleisure-trend-is-here-to-stay/#674c955528bd, accessed August 2, 2017.

3. Douglas Coupland, *Generation X: Tales for an Accelerated Culture*, St. Martin's Griffin, 1991.

4. Alladi Venkatesh, "Postmodernism, Poststructuralism and Marketing," paper presented at the American Marketing Association Winter Theory Conference, San Antonio, Texas, February 1992; see also Stella Proctor, Ioanna Papasolomou-Doukakis, and Tony Proctor, "What are Television Advertisements Really Trying to Tell Us? A Postmodern Perspective," *Journal of Consumer Behavior* 1 (February 2002): 246–255; A. Fuat Firat, "The Consumer in Postmodernity," in NA: Advances in Consumer Research, eds. Rebecca H. Holman and Michael R. Solomon (1991), Vol. 18, Provo, UT: Association for Consumer Research: 70-76.

5. Miriam Jordan, "India Decides to Put Its Own Spin on Popular Rock, Rap and Reggae," *Wall Street Journal* (January 5, 2000), www.wsj.com, accessed January 5, 2000; Rasul Bailay, "Coca-Cola Recruits Paraplegics for 'Cola War' in India," *Wall Street Journal* (June 10, 1997).

6. Russell W. Belk, "Third World Consumer Culture," *Research in Marketing*, JAI Press: Greenwich, CT, 1988: 103-127.

7. Rick Wartzman, "When You Translate 'Got Milk' for Latinos, What Do You Get?" *Wall Street Journal* (June 3, 1999).

8. Russell W. Belk, "Third World Consumer Culture," *Research in Marketing*, JAI Press: Greenwich, CT, 1988: 103-127.

9. Karlene Lukovitz, "Coffee Marketers Need to Woo Young Adults," *Marketing Daily* (October 8, 2010), http://www.mediapost.com/

publications/? fa=Articles.showArticle&art_aid=137318, accessed April 29, 2011.

10. Benny Barak and Leon G. Schiffman, "Cognitive Age: A Nonchronological Age Variable," in Kent B. Monroe, ed., *Advances in Consumer Research* 8 (Provo, UT: Association for Consumer Research, 1981): 602–6.

11. Stephen Holden, "After the War the Time of the Teen-Ager," *New York Times* (May 7, 1995): E4.

12. Jennings, "Contests, YouTube and Commercials Converge for Skin Product"; cf. also Szmigin and Carrigan, "Consumption and Community: Choices for Women Over Forty."

13. John H. Fleming, "Baby Boomers Are Opening Their Wallets," *Gallup Business Journal* (January 30, 2015), http://www.gallup.com/businessjournal/181367/baby-boomers-opening-wallets.aspx, accessed April 21, 2015.

14. Quoted in Sarah Mahoney, "Nielsen: Time to Recommit to Boomers," *Marketing Daily* (July 21, 2010), http://www.mediapost.com/publications/article/132364/nielsen-time-to-recommit-to-boomers.html?edition=, accessed April 21, 2015.

15. Hiawatha Bray, "At MIT's AgeLab Growing Old Is the New Frontier," *Boston Globe* (March 23, 2009), www.boston.com/business/technology/articles/2009/03/23/at_mits_agelab_growing_old_is_the_new_frontier/?s_campaign=8315, accessed March 23, 2009.

16. D'Vera Cohn, "2100 Census Forecast: Minorities Expected to Account for 60% of U.S. Population," *Washington Post* (January 13, 2000): A5.

17. Catherine A. Cole and Nadine N. Castellano, "Consumer Behavior," in James E. Binnen, ed., *Encyclopedia of Gerontology*, vol. 1 (San Diego, CA: Academic Press, 1996), 329–39.

18. Rick Adler, "Stereotypes Won't Work with Seniors Anymore," *Advertising Age* (November 11, 1996): 32.

19. Hope Jensen Schau, Mary C. Gilly, and Mary Wolfinbarger, "Consumer Identity Renaissance: The Resurgence of Identity-Inspired Consumption in Retirement," *Journal of Consumer Research* 36 (August 2009): 255–76; cf. also Michelle Barnhart and Lisa Peñaloza, "Who Are You Calling Old? Negotiating Old Age Identity in the Elderly Consumption Ensemble," *Journal of Consumer Research* (April 2013), 39, 6: 1133-1153.

20. "Race Becomes More Central to TV Advertising," http://www.nbcnews.com/id/29453960/ns/business-us_business/t/race-becomes-more-central-tv-advertising/ (March 1, 2009), accessed August 7, 2017.

21. Michelle Castillo, "Study: Americans want more diversity in ads," (March 7, 2016), https://www.cnbc.com/2016/03/07/study-americans-want-more-diversity-in-ads.html, accessed August 8, 2017.

22. Tim Nudd, "Ad of the Day: Cheerios Brings Back Its Famous Interracial Family for the Super Bowl," *Adweek* (January 29, 2014), http://www.adweek.com/brand-marketing/ad-day-cheerios-brings-back-its-famous-interracial-family-super-bowl-155302/, accessed October 15, 2017.

23. http://www.pewresearch.org/fact-tank/2014/03/14/u-s-census-looking-at-big-changes-in-how-it-asks-about-race-and-ethnicity/, accessed November 17, 2017.

24. Michael Cooper, "Census Officials, Citing Increasing Diversity, Say U.S. Will Be a 'Plurality Nation,'" *New York Times* (December 12, 2012), http://www.nytimes.com/2012/12/13/us/us-will-have-no-ethnic-majority-census-finds.html, accessed February 18, 2015; Susan Saulny, "Census Data Presents Rise in Multiracial Population of Youths," *New York Times* (March 24, 2011), http://www.nytimes.com/2011/03/25/us/25race.html?_r=2&ref=census, accessed April 24, 2011.

25. Some of the content has been adapted from Rachel Ashman, Michael R. Solomon and Julia Wolny, "An Old Model for a New Age: Applying the EKB in Today's Participatory Culture," *Journal of Customer Behaviour*, 2015, 14(2): 127-146.

26. James F. Engel, David T. Kollat and Roger D. Blackwell, *Consumer Behavior*, New York: Holt, Rinehart and Winston, 1968; https://books.

google.com/books/about/Consumer_behavior.html?id=3ta2r-. accessed October 13, 2017.D2XesC

27. Quoted from Jim Lecinski, *Winning the Zero Moment of Truth*, Google (2011), file:///Users/msolom01/Dropbox/2011-winning-zmot-ebook research-studies.pdf, accessed July 6, 2017.

28. For one recent, somewhat similar perspective cf. Jamie Turner, Reshma Shah and Varsha Jain, *How Brands are Using Nonlinear Marketing to Connect with Customers in the Post-Advertising Era*, 60 Second Marketer, Atlanta: 2018.

29. Aaron Smith and Monica Anderson, "Online Shopping and E-Commerce," Pew Research Center (December 19, 2016), http://www.pewInternet.org/2016/12/19/online-shopping-and-e-commerce/, accessed July 6, 2017.

30. Maria Konnikova, "How Facebook Makes Us Unhappy," *The New Yorker* (September 10, 2013), http://www.newyorker.com/tech/elements/how-facebook-makes-us-unhappy, accessed July 1, 2017.

31. Ginny Marvin, "Report: Google Earns 78% Of $36.7B US Search Ad Revenues, Soon to be 80%," *Search Engine Land*, March 14, 2017, http://searchengineland.com/google-search-ad-revenues-271188, accessed July 1, 2017.

32. https://www.onblastblog.com/blog-teenagers-5-young-fashion-bloggers-follow/, accessed November 19, 2017.

33. "Fashion Retailers Eye Up Image-Recognition Apps for Smartphones," *The Guardian* (April 20, 2014), https://www.theguardian.com/business/2014/apr/20/fashion-retailers-image-recognition-apps-smartphones, accessed July 4, 2017.

34. Eli Pariser, *The Filter Bubble: How the New Personalized Web Is Changing What We Read and How We Think*, New York: Penguin Books, 2012.

35. Sarah Perez, "79 Percent Of Americans Now Shop Online, But It's Cost More than Convenience that Sways Them," *Techcrunch* (December 19, 2016), https://techcrunch.

36. com/2016/12/19/79-percent-of-americans-now-shop-online-but-its-cost-more-than-convenience-that-sways-them/, accessed July 1, 2017.

36. Kimberlee Morrison, "81% of Shoppers Conduct Online Research Before Buying," *Adweek* (November 28, 2014), http://www.adweek.com/digital/81-shoppers-conduct-online-research-making-purchase-infographic/, accessed July 1, 2017.

37. Christian Jarrett, "How Food Porn Hijacks Your Brain," *New York Times Magazine* (October 20, 2015), http://nymag.com/scienceofus/2015/10/how-food-porn-hijacks-your-brain.html, accessed July 5, 2017.

38. Carol F. Surprenant and Michael R. Solomon (1987), "Predictability and Personalization in the Service Encounter," *Journal of Marketing*, 51 (April), 8696.

39. www.forrest.com/customer-journey, accessed November 19, 2017.

40. https://theleadershipnetwork.com/article/lean-manufacturing/gemba-walk, accessed November 19, 2017.

41. https://www.amazon.com/s/ref=nb_sb_ss_i_1_17?url=search-alias%3Daps&field-keywords=solomon+consumer+behavior+12th+edition&sprefix=solomon+consumer+%2Caps%2C170&crid=3P1UXFOHASC3F, accessed November 19, 2017.

42. https://hbr.org/2016/03/what-you-can-and-should-be-doing-with-your-customer-journeys, accessed November 19, 2017.

43. Cf. Tracy Tuten and Michael R. Solomon, *Social Media Marketing* 3rd ed., London: Sage, 2019.

44. https://www.omnicoreagency.com/facebook-statistics/, accessed November 26, 2017.

45. Robert Putnam, *Bowling Alone: The Collapse and Revival of American Community*, New York: Touchstone Books, 2001.

46. Tracy Tuten and Michael R. Solomon, *Social Media Marketing* 2nd ed., London: SAGE, 2016.

47. *Bazaarvoice,* 2013

48. "125 Amazing Social Media Statistics You Should Know in 2016," *Social Pilot,* https://socialpilot.co/blog/125-amazing-social-media-statistics-know-2016/, accessed July 5, 2017.

49. Bob Al-Greene, "Late-Night Gadget Use Damages Your Sleep Cycle," *Mashable* (November 19, 2012), http://mashable.com/2012/11/19/-gadgets-sleep/, accessed July 5, 2017.

50. Quoted in http://www.businessinsider.com/how-uber-and-lyft-drivers-decide-your-passenger-rating-2016-10, accessed November 21, 2017.

51. "The Human Brain is Loaded Daily with 34 GB of Information," *Tech 21 Century,* http://www.tech21century.com/the-human-brain-is-loaded-daily-with-34-gb-of-information/, accessed July 12, 2017.

52. Jennifer Lai, "Information Wants to be Free ... and Expensive," *Forbes* (July 20, 2009), http://fortune.com/2009/07/20/information-wants-to-be-free-and-expensive/, accessed July 13, 2017.

53. Quoted in E.J. Schultz, "How 'Crash the Super Bowl' Changed Advertising," *Advertising Age* (January 4, 2016), http://adage.com/article/special-report-super-bowl/crash-super-bowl-changed-advertising/301966/, accessed July 13, 2017.

54. Richard A. Peterson and D. G. Berger, "Entrepreneurship in Organizations: Evidence from the Popular Music Industry," *Administrative Science Quarterly* 16 (1971): 97–107.

55. *Ben Sisario,* "In Beyoncé Deal, Pepsi Focuses on Collaboration," *New York Times* (December 9, 2012), http://www.nytimes.com/2012/12/10/business/media/in-beyonce-deal-pepsi-focuses-on-collaboration.html?smid=tw-nytimesmusic&seid=auto&_r=1&, accessed February 16, 2013.

56. Paul M. Hirsch, "Processing Fads and Fashions: An Organizational Set Analysis of Cultural Industry Systems," *American Journal of Sociology* 77, no. 4 (1972): 639–659; Russell Lynes, *The Tastemakers* (New York: Harper & Brothers, 1954); Michael R. Solomon, "The Missing Link: Surrogate

Consumers in the Marketing Chain," *Journal of Marketing* 50 (October 1986): 208–219.

57. Elaine Glusac, "Meet Your New Data-Driven Travel Agent," *New York Times* (July 10, 2017), https://www.nytimes.com/2017/07/10/travel/meet-your-next-travel-agent-diy-artificial-intelligence.html?emc=eta1, accessed July 15, 2017.

58. Stuart M. Butler, "How Google and Coursera May Upend the Traditional College Degree," *Brookings* (October 23, 2015), https://www.brookings.edu/blog/techtank/2015/02/23/how-google-and-coursera-may-upend-the-traditional-college-degree/, accessed July 14, 2017.

59. Adapted from Rachel Ashman, Kristhy Salazar, and Michael Solomon, "Let's Go Social Shopping! Social Shopping in a Researcher's Paradise," Institute of Direct and Digital Marketing, Google UK, January 2014.

60. Barbara Thau, "Five Signs That Stores (Not E-Commerce) Are The Future Of Retail," *Forbes* (June 27, 2017), https://www.forbes.com/sites/barbarathau/2017/06/27/five-signs-that-stores-not-online-shopping-are-the-future-of-retail/#27d057f04641, accessed September 23, 2017.

61. Evan Asano, "How Much Time Do People Spend on Social Media?," *Social Media Today* (January 4, 2017), http://www.socialmediatoday.com/marketing/how-much-time-do-people-spend-social-media-infographic, accessed September 23, 2017.

62. Natalie Wood, Michael R. Solomon and David Allan (2008), "Welcome to the Matrix: E-Learning gets a Second Life," *Marketing Education Review* 18 (2), 1-7; Natalie Wood, Lyle R. Wetsch, Michael R. Solomon and Ken Hudson (2009), "From Interactive to Immersive: Advertising Education takes a Virtual Leap of Faith." *Journal of Advertising Education*, 13 (1), 64-72.

63. Jon Brouchoud,"Construction of aLoft's Flagship Hotels, First Prototyped In Second Life, Now Complete," *Arch Virtual* (June 24, 2010), http://archvirtual.com/2010/06/24/construction-of-alofts-flagship-hotels-first-prototyped-in-second-life-now-complete/, accessed September 30, 2017.

64. Ben Lang, "'Sansar' Will Open to All in First Half of 2017 with a New Approach to Virtual Worlds," *Road to VR* (January 15, 2017), https://www.roadtovr.com/sansar-release-date-preview-virtual-reality-liden-lab/, accessed September 23, 2017.

65. http://www.thesuccessalliance.com/what-is-a-mastermind-group/, accessed December 2, 2017.

66. Natalie T Wood, Michael R. Solomon, Greg W. Marshall and Sarah Lincoln (2010), Corporate Education Goes Virtual: A Hybrid Approach to Experiential Learning, in *Handbook of Research on Virtual Environments for Corporate Education: Employee Learning and Solutions* ed. William F. Ritke-Jones, Hershey, PA: IGI Global.

67. Joe Tenebruso, "21 Video Game Stats That Will Blow You Away," *The Motley Fool* (February 25, 2017), https://www.fool.com/investing/2017/02/25/21-video-game-stats-that-will-blow-you-away.aspx, accessed September 23, 2017.

68. Susan Borst, "Forecast 2017: Brands To Take A Fresh Look At Game Advertising," Interactive Advertising Bureau (November 11, 2016), https://www.iab.com/news/forecast-2017-brands-take-fresh-look-game-advertising/, accessed September 23, 2017.

69. Tracy Tuten and Michael R. Solomon, *Social Media Marketing*, 3rd ed., London: SAGE, 2019.

70. https://www.theguardian.com/sport/2017/jun/16/top-addiction-young-people-gaming-esports, accessed November 21, 2017.

71. Brent Conrad, "Computer Game Addiction - Symptoms, Treatment, & FAQs," *Tech Addiction*, http://www.techaddiction.ca/computer_game_addiction.html, accessed September 25, 2017.

72. Samantha Murphy Kelly, "Job Site Wants Only Beautiful Candidates," *Mashable* (June 2, 2013), http://mashable.com/2013/06/02/beautiful-people-job-site/?WT.mc_id=en_my_stories&utm_campaign=My%2BStories&utm_medium=email&utm_source=newsletter, accessed January 30, 2015.

73. Daniel S. Hamermesh, "Ugly? You May Have a Case," *New York Times Magazine* (August 27, 2011), http://www.nytimes.com/2011/08/28/opinion/sunday/ugly-you-may-have-a-case.html?ref=opinion, accessed March 22, 2015.

74. Lois W. Banner, *American Beauty* (Chicago: University of Chicago Press, 1980); for a philosophical perspective, see Barry Vacker and Wayne R. Key, "Beauty and the Beholder: The Pursuit of Beauty Through Commodities," *Psychology & Marketing* 10 (November–December 1993): 471–494.

75. https://www.theguardian.com/lifeandstyle/2014/dec/17/kim-kardashian-butt-break-the-internet-paper-magazine, accessed December 2, 2017; https://www.self.com/story/butt-enhancement-surgery-is-way-more-popular-than-you-thought, accessed December 2, 2017.

76. https://www.nbcnews.com/better/health/how-beauty-standard-has-changed-1990-how-it-hasn-t-ncna809766, accessed December 2, 2017.

77. "The Big Business Of Red Carpet Bling," *Fast Company* (September 18, 2016).

78. Adapted from Jagdish N. Sheth and Michael R. Solomon, "Extending the Extended Self in a Digital World," *Journal of Marketing Theory and Practice*, 2014, Volume 22, Number 2: 123-132; cf. also Russell W. Belk (2013), "Extended Self in a Digital World," *Journal of Consumer Research*, 40(3), 477-500.

79. https://www.thesun.co.uk/living/2651730/ever-wondered-why-some-mirrors-make-you-look-skinnier-than-others-heres-the-reason/, accessed November 21, 2017.

80. Andrew Rosenblum, "2015: The Year Virtual Reality Finally Reaches Living Rooms," *Popular Science* (January 12, 2015), http://www.popsci.com/virtual-reality-meets-its-public, accessed March 9, 2015.

81. Chuck Martin, "Hershey's Taps VR To Test In-Store Marketing, Mediapost.com," Mediapost.com (July 10, 2017), https://www.mediapost.com/publications/article/304046/hersheys-taps-vr-to-test-in-store-marketing.html?utm_source=newsletter&utm_medium=email&utm_

content=readnow&utm_campaign=104136&hashid=eVVwVNz5JMib0 Noa-eSr9QuVlK0, accessed September 29, 2017.

82. Deniz Ergürel, "Amazon is Building Virtual and Augmented Reality Stores,", *Haptic.AL*, (March 26, 2017), https://haptic.al/amazon-virtual-store-, 33c420b5f921, accessed September 29, 2017.

83. Nicola K Smith, "How virtual reality is shaking up the music industry," *BBC News* (January 31, 2017), http://www.bbc.com/news/business-38795190, accessed September 29, 2017.

84. Brooks Barnes, "Coming Soon to AMC Theaters: Virtual Reality Experiences," *New York Times* (September 26, 2017), https://www.nytimes.com/2017/09/26/business/media/amc-theaters-virtual-reality.html, accessed September 27, 2017.

85. Cf. for example Fox, J., Bailenson, J.N., & Tricase, L. (2013). The Embodiment of Sexualized Virtual Selves: The Proteus Effect and Experiences of Self-Objectification via Avatars. *Computers in Human Behavior. 29*, 930-938.

86. Fox, Jesse; Bailenson, Jeremy N. (2009). "Virtual Self-Modeling: The Effects of Vicarious Reinforcement and Identification on Exercise Behaviors". *Media Psychology.* 12(1): 1–25.

87. Messinger, Paul R.; Ge, Xin; Stroulia, Eleni; Lyons, Kelly; Smirnov, Kristen; Bone, Michael (November 2008). "On the Relationship between My Avatar and Myself," *Journal of Virtual Worlds Research*. 1 (2): 1–17.

88. The Best Costumes We've Seen at San Diego Comic-Con So Far," *Fortune* (July 21, 2017), http://fortune.com/2017/07/21/san-diego-comic-con-2017-photos/, accessed September 30, 2017.

89. "Nearly 1 in 5 People Have a Disability in the U.S., Census Bureau Reports," U.S. Census Bureau (July 25, 2012), https://www.census.gov/newsroom/releases/archives/miscellaneous/cb12-134.html, accessed March 5, 2015; Susannah Fox, "Americans Living with Disability and Their Technology Profile," *PewInternet* (January 21, 2011), http://pewinternet.org/Reports/2011/Disability.aspx, accessed January 2, 2013; Terry L. Childers and Carol Kaufman-Scarborough, "Expanding

Opportunities for Online Shoppers with Disabilities," *Journal of Business Research* 62 (2009), 572–578.

90. Michael R. Solomon, Kel Smith, Nadine Vogel, and Natalie T. Wood, "Virtual Freedom for People with Disabilities," *Society for Disability Studies, Philadelphia* (June 2010).

91. Daisy Dunne, "Could THIS Improve Inflight Customer Service? Airline Tests 'Mixed Reality' Hololens Glasses to Attend to Passengers' Needs," *Daily Mail*, (May 25, 2017), http://www.dailymail.co.uk/sciencetech/article-4540930/Flight-attendants-use-Microsoft-HoloLens-customers.html#ixzz4u6X2dKHr, accessed September 29, 2017.

92. http://www.microsoft.com/microsoft-hololens/en-us, accessed March 9, 2015.

93. Gabriel Kahn, "Chinese Characters Are Gaining New Meaning as Corporate Logos," *Wall Street Journal Interactive Edition* (July 18, 2002).

94. Natalie Zmuda, "Why Tommy Hilfiger Boosted Ad Budget by 60%, Aired First Branded TV Spot Since 2005," *Ad Age CMO Strategy*, http://adage.com/article/cmo-strategy/marketing-tommy-hilfiger-boosted-ad-budget-60/147258/, accessed April 28, 2011.

95. Matt Weinberger, "Augmented Reality is Already Changing the Way Big Companies Do Business," *Business Insider* (June 26, 2017), http://www.businessinsider.com/augmented-reality-in-the-enterprise-2017-6, accessed September 29, 2017.

96. Margaret Rhodes, "How A Beauty Startup Turned Instagram Comments Into A Product Line," *Wired* (November 26, 2014), https://Www.Wired.Com/2014/11/Beauty-Startup-Turned-Instagram-Comments-Product-Line/, accessed September 30, 2017.

97. Sam Milbrath, "Co-Creation: 5 Examples of Brands Driving Customer-Driven Innovation," *Vision Critical* (August 5, 2016), https://www.visioncritical.com/5-examples-how-brands-are-using-co-creation/, accessed October 2, 2017.

98. Hidehiko Nishikawa, Martin Schreier and Susumu Ogaw, "User-Generated Versus Designer-Generated Products: A Performance Assessment at Muji," *International Journal of Research in Marketing*, Volume 30, Issue 2, June 2013:160-167, http://www.sciencedirect.com/science/article/pii/S0167811612000730, accessed September 30, 2017.

99. https://www.redchiliclimbing.com/en/, accessed October 2, 2017.

100. https://www.threadless.com/how-it-works/, accessed October 2, 2017.

101. James Surowiecki, *The Wisdom of Crowds: Why the Many Are Smarter Than the Few and How Collective Wisdom Shapes Business, Economies, Societies and Nations*, 2004, New York: Doubleday.

102. Adam Mann, "The Power of Prediction Markets," *Nature* (October 18, 2016), https://www.nature.com/news/the-power-of-prediction-markets-1.20820, accessed September 30, 2017; Julie Wittes Schlack, Ask Your Customers for Predictions, Not Preferences," *Harvard Business Review* (January 5, 2015), https://hbr.org/2015/01/ask-your-customers-for-predictions-not-preferences, accessed September 30, 2017.

103. https://tippie.biz.uiowa.edu/iem/, accessed December 2, 2017.

104. Barbara Kiviat, "The End of Management," *Time Inside Business* (July 12, 2004), www.time.com/time/magazine/article/0,9171,994658,00.html, accessed October 5, 2007.

105. "DIY Home Improvement Market in the US 2017-2021," *PR Newswire* (May 4, 2017), http://www.prnewswire.com/news-releases/diy-home-improvement-market-in-the-us-2017-2021-300451798.html, accessed September 30, 2017.

106. Nicholas Jackson, "7 Successful Products to Emerge from San Francisco's Techshop," *The Atlantic* (July 5, 2011), theatlantic.Com/Technology/Archive/2011/07/7-Successful-Products-To-Emerge-From-San-Franciscos-Techshop/241291/#Slide4, accessed September 30, 2017; "What Is A Makerspace?," *Makerspaces.com*, https://www.Makerspaces.Com/What-Is-A-Makerspace/, accessed September 30, 2017.

107. Julie Napoli, Sonia J. Dickinson, Michael B. Beverland and Francis Farrelly, "Measuring Consumer-Based Brand Authenticity," *Journal of Business Research* 67, no. 6 (2014): 1090–1098.

108. George E. Newman and Ravi Dhar, "Authenticity Is Contagious: Brand Essence and the Original Source of Production," *Journal of Marketing Research* 51, no. 3 (2014): 371–386; Quoted in Matthew Hutson, "Quenching Consumers' Thirst for 'Authentic' Brands," *New York Times*, (December 27, 2014), http://www.nytimes.com/2014/12/28/business/quenching-consumers-thirst-for-authentic-brands.html?module=Search&mabReward=relbias%3Ar%2C%7B%221%22%3-A%22RI%3A11%22%7D&_r=0, accessed February 18, 2015; George E. Newman and Ravi Dhar, "Authenticity is Contagious: Brand Essence and the Original Source of Production," *Journal of Marketing Research* 51 (June 2014): 371–386.

109. John Winsor, "The End of Traditional Ad Agencies," *Harvard Business Review* (May 9, 2013), https://hbr.org/2013/05/the-end-of-traditional-ad-agen, accessed October 2, 2017.

110. Travis Wright, "Why Brands Should Embrace UGC as Part of Their Marketing Strategy," *Marketing Land* (February 13, 2017), https://marketingland.com/ugc-brands-new-years-content-resolution-2017-206106, accessed September 20, 2017.

111. "People Trust Social Media Photos 7 Times More than Traditional Ads," *Net Imperative* (November 30, 2016), http://www.netimperative.com/2016/11/people-trust-social-media-photos-7-times-traditional-ads-report/, accessed September 30, 2017.

112. Blair Evan Bell, "How Blogs Influence Your Purchase Decisions [Infographic], *Prepare1.com* (February 13, 2015), https://www.prepare1.com/blogs-influence-purchase-decisions/, accessed October 2, 2017.

113. Wendy Koch, "'Green' Product Claims Are Often Misleading," *USA Today* (October 26, 2010), http://content.usatoday.com/communities/greenhouse/post/2010/10/green-product-claims/1?csp=34money&utm_source=feedburner&utm_medium=feed&utm_campaign=Feed%3A+Us

atodaycomMoney-TopStories+%28Money+-+Top+Stories%29, accessed April 10, 2011.

114. http://adage.com/article/media/marketers-media-trusts/298221/, accessed November 26, 2017.

115. https://www.usatoday.com/story/tech/news/2017/11/16/facebook-google-twitter-and-media-outlets-fight-fake-news-trust-indicators/869200001/, accessed November 26, 2017.

116. http://mashable.com/2017/11/16/facebook-trust-indicators-fake-news-problem/#MEZcLBccUZq4, accessed November 26, 2017.

117. https://www.forbes.com/sites/joshsteimle/2014/09/19/what-is-content-marketing/#6c5464da10b9, accessed November 26, 2017.

118. Kim Severson, "Inspiring Mayberry, and Then Becoming It," *New York Times* (June 21, 2013), http://www.New York Times.com/2013/06/22/us/in-north-carolina-inspiring-mayberry-and-then-becoming-it.html?_r=0, accessed February 23, 2015.

119. Hellen Lundell, "Fictional Food: Consumers Taking the Lead on Food Fabrication," *Heartbeat* (June 18, 2013), http://www.hartman-group.com/hartbeat/fictional-foodconsumers-taking--the-lead-on-food fabrication?utm_content=msolom01@sju.edu&tm_keyword=1fM92wXkAvpCt0zU6Ab&utm_source=tailoretmail&utm_term=Read+More%26nbsp%3b-%C2%BB&utm_campaign=Fictional+food%2c+fad+or+fantasy%3f&tm_campaign=FICTIONAL+FOOD+CONSUMERS+TAKING+THE+LEAD+ON+FOOD+FABRICATION&, accessed February 23, 2015.

120. Dale Buss, "The GEICO Gecko Finds his Voice—and Puts it Into Book About Being 'Human'" *Brand Channel* (April 25, 2013), http://www.brandchannel.com/home/post/2013/04/25/Geico-Gecko-Book-042513.aspx, accessed February 23, 2015.

121. Mark J. Miller, "Nike Pulls Tattoo-Inspired Line After Outcry from Samoan Community," *Brandchannel* (August 15, 2013), http://www.brandchannel.com/home/post/2013/08/15/Nike-Pulls-Tattoo-Line-081514.aspx, accessed February 16, 2015.

[122.] http://americanhistory.si.edu/press/fact-sheets/ruby-slippers, accessed April 23, 2015; George E. Newman, Gil Diesendruck, and Paul Bloom, "Celebrity Contagion and the Value of Objects," *Journal of Consumer Research* 38, no. 2 (August 2011): 215–228.

[123.] http://schools.walkerart.org/swita/switaact8.html, accessed December 3, 2017.

[124.] Howard S. Becker, "Arts and Crafts," *American Journal of Sociology* 83 (January 1987): 862–889.

[125.] Herbert J. Gans, "Popular Culture in America: Social Problem in a Mass Society or Social Asset in a Pluralist Society?" in Howard S. Becker, ed., *Social Problems: A Modern Approach* (New York: Wiley, 1966).

[126.] Annetta Miller, "Shopping Bags Imitate Art: Seen the Sacks? Now Visit the Museum Exhibit," *Newsweek* (January 23, 1989): 44.

[127.] Kim Foltz, "New Species for Study: Consumers in Action," *New York Times* (December 18, 1989): A1.

[128.] Susan Birrell, "Sports as Ritual: Interpretations from Durkheim to Goffman," *Social Forces* 60, no. 2 (1981): 354–376; Daniel Q. Voigt, "American Sporting Rituals," in Browne, ed., *Rites and Ceremonies in Popular Culture*.

[129.] Ronald W. Pimentel and Kristy E. Reynolds, "A Model for Consumer Devotion: Affective Commitment with Proactive Sustaining Behaviors," *Academy of Marketing Science Review* 5 (2004): 1.

[130.] Dean MacCannell, *The Tourist: A New Theory of the Leisure Class* (New York: Shocken Books, 1976).

[131.] Deborah Hofmann, "In Jewelry, Choices Sacred and Profane, Ancient and New," *New York Times* (May 7, 1989), www.nytimes.com, accessed October 11, 2007.

[132.] https://www.packagedfacts.com/Religious-Publishing-Products-1692979/, accessed December 3, 2017.

133. https://www.ebayinc.com/our-company/who-we-are/, accessed September 30, 2017.

134. http://www.dsa.org/docs/default-source/research/growth-outlook/dsa_2016gandofactsheet.pdf?sfvrsn=2, accessed September 30, 2017.

135. http://www.dsa.org/docs/default-source/direct-selling-facts/internalconsumptionfacts.pdf?sfvrsn=2, accessed December 2, 2017.

136. "Uber, Airbnb Lead the Way as Sharing Economy Expands," *emarketer.com* (June 30, 2017), https://www.emarketer.com/Article/Uber-Airbnb-Lead-Way-Sharing-Economy-Expands/1016109, accessed September 30, 2017.

137. Greg Gardner, "Report: More New Cars Leased Than Ever," *USA Today* (March 4, 2016), https://www.usatoday.com/story/money/cars/2016/03/03/report-more-new-cars-leased-than-ever/81286732/, accessed September 30, 2017.

138. https://www.bookbycadillac.com/#benefits-slide2, accessed October 3, 2017.

139. https://www.inc.com/magazine/201707/zoe-henry/jennifer-fleiss-rent-the-runway.html, accessed November 26, 2017.

140. Julie Beck, "The Decline of the Driver's License," *The Atlantic* (January 22, 2016), https://www.theatlantic.com/technology/archive/2016/01/the-decline-of-the-drivers-license/425169/, accessed September 30, 2017.

141. "Number of People Using Zipcar as Car Rental Company Within the Last 12 Months in The United States from Spring 2008 To Spring 2017 (In Thousands)," *Statista* https://www.statista.com/statistics/295919/zipcar-customers-usa/, accessed October 3, 2017.

142. John Gray, *Men Are from Mars, Women Are from Venus: Practical Guide for Improving Communication*, New York: HarperCollins, 2009.

143. Comprehensive* List of LGBTQ+ Vocabulary Definitions, http://itspronouncedmetrosexual.com/2013/01/a-comprehensive-list-of-lgbtq-term-definitions/, accessed August 7, 2017.

144. Diane Goldner, "What Men and Women Really Want . . . to Eat," *New York Times* (March 2, 1994): C1(2).

145. Paul Rozin, Julia M. Hormes. Myles S. Faith, and Brian Wansink, "Is Meat Male?: A Quantitative Multimethod Framework to Establish Metaphoric Relationships," *Journal of Consumer Research* 39, no. 3 (2012): 629–643.

146. Sarah Mahoney, "Study: Men's Mags May Be Bad For Men," *Marketing Daily* (March 2, 2013), http://www.mediapost.com/publications/article/194617/study-mens-mags-may-be-bad-for-men.html?edition=57304#axzz2MuwUQkdG, accessed February 25, 2015.

147. Quoted in Natalie Zmuda, "Can Dr Pepper's Mid-Cal Soda Score a 10 with Men?" *Advertising Age* (February 21, 2011), http://adage.com/article/news/dr-pepper-10-avoid-marketing-missteps-pepsi-coke/148983/, accessed April 10, 2011.

148. Sandra L. Bem, "The Measurement of Psychological Androgyny," *Journal of Consulting & Clinical Psychology* 42 (1974): 155–162; Deborah E. S. Frable, "Sex Typing and Gender Ideology: Two Facets of the Individual's Gender Psychology That Go Together," *Journal of Personality & Social Psychology* 56, no. 1 (1989): 95–108.

149. Susan Chira, "When Japan Had a Third Gender," *New York Times* (March 10, 2017), https://www.nytimes.com/2017/03/10/arts/design/when-japan-had-a-third-gender.html?_r=0, accessed October 4, 2017.

150. Geoffrey A. Fowler, "Asia's Lipstick Lads," *Wall Street Journal* (May 27, 2005), www.wsj.com, accessed May 27, 2005.

151. Matt Alt and Hiroko Yoda, "Big Primpin' in Tokyo," *Wired* (May 2007): 46.

152. Quoted in https://www.canvas8.com/signals/2017/12/07/balenciaga-mixes-collections.html, accessed December 7, 2017.

153. Nic Screws, "Men's Fashion Is Headed for a Gender-Bending Moment Unseen Since the '70s," Bloomburg Pursuits (August 6, 2015), https://www.bloomberg.com/news/articles/2015-08-06/men-s-fashion-is-headed-for-a-gender-bending-moment-unseen-since-the-70s, accessed October 3, 2017.

154. Rupal Parekh, "Gender-Bending Brands an Easy Way to Increase Product Reach," *Advertising Age* (March 2, 2009), www.adage.com, accessed March 24, 2015; Sarah Mahoney, "Best Buy Opens Store Designed for Women," *Retail Customer Experience* (October 6, 2008), http://www.retailcustomerexperience.com/news/best-buy-opens-store-designed-for-women/, accessed March 24, 2015; Kevin Helliker, "The Solution to Hunting's Woes? Setting Sights on Women," *Wall Street Journal* (October 1, 2008), http://online.wsj.com/Article/Sb122281550760292225.Html?Mod=Dist_Smartbrief, accessed October 2, 2008; Stephanie Clifford, "Frito-Lay Tries to Enter the Minds (and Lunch Bags) of Women," *New York Times* (February 24, 2009), http://www.nytimes.com/2009/02/25/business/media/25adco.html?, accessed March 24, 2015; Karl Greenberg, "Harley Says Guys Ride Back Seat in May," *Marketing Daily* (February 3, 2009), www.mediapost.com, accessed February 3, 2009.

155. Julie Creswell, "American Girl's New Doll: It's a Boy!," *New York Times* (February 14, 2017), https://www.nytimes.com/2017/02/14/business/american-girls-new-doll-its-a-boy.html?_r=0, accessed October 4, 2017.

156. Lauren Coleman-Lochner, "Old Spice Attracting Women in Gender-Bending Hit for P&G," *Bloomburg Business* (March 12, 2015), http://www.bloomberg.com/news/articles/2014-03-12/old-spice-attracting-women-in-gender-bending-hit-for-p-g, accessed March 20, 2015.

157. Quoted in Elizabeth Segran, "Women's Tighty Whities and Men's Hot Pink Briefs: Gender-Bending Fashion Goes Mainstream," *Fast Company* (September 19, 2016), https://www.fastcompany.com/3062838/womens-tighty-whities-and-mens-hot-pink-briefs-gender-bending-fashion-goes-m, accessed October 4, 2017.

158. "Mmuk Man: Putting the Guy in Guyliner," *Canvas8* (June 5, 2015), https://www.Canvas8.Com/Content/2015/06/05/Mmuk.Html, accessed October 4, 2017.

159. For an academic study of this subculture, cf. Steven M. Kates, "The Dynamics of Brand Legitimacy: An Interpretive Study in the Gay Men's Community," *Journal of Consumer Research* 31 (September 2004): 455–464.

160. Julia Baird, "Neither Female Nor Male," *New York Times* (April 6, 2014), http://www.nytimes.com/2014/04/07/opinion/neither-female-nor-male.html?ref=opinion, accessed February 21, 2015.

161. https://www.cnn.com/2017/10/17/politics/governor-jerry-brown-california-law-nonbinary/index.html, accessed November 26, 2017.

162. Martha Mendoza, "Facebook Adds New Gender Options for Users," *NBC New York*, http://www.nbcnewyork.com/news/national-international/Facebook-Gender-Options--245407751.html, accessed October 4, 2017.

163. Matthew Chapman, "Benetton to Feature Trans-Sexual Brazilian Model in Spring/Summer Campaign," *marketingmagazine.co.uk* (January 23, 2013), http://www.brandrepublic.com/news/1168021/Benetton-feature-trans-sexual-Brazilian-model-Spring-Summer-campaign/, accessed February 21, 2015.

164. Marjorie Garber (25 November 1997). *Vested Interests: Cross-dressing and Cultural Anxiety*. Psychology Press. pp. 2, 10, 14–16, 47. .

165. Jacob Hodes and Emma Ruby-Sachs, "'America's Army' Targets Youth," *The Nation* (August 23, 2002), https://archive.is/20081202184214/http://www.thenation.com/doc/20020902/hodes20020823#selection-469.0-487.15, accessed October 10, 2017.

166. "Thirty-Five Percent of Americans Shop Online While at Work, Says FindLaw.com Survey," ThomsonReuters.com (November 26, 2014), https://www.thomsonreuters.com/en/press-releases/2014/thirty-five-percent-of-americans-shop-online-while-at-work-says-findlaw-com-survey.html, accessed October 15, 2017.

167. https://www.nytimes.com/2017/02/15/us/remote-workers-work-from-home.html?_r=0, accessed December 2, 2017.

168. Jamie Carson, "10 Suits to Wear Outside the Office," *Shortlist.com* (July 8, 2016), https://www.shortlist.com/style/fashion/10-suits-to-wear-outside-the-office/28329, accessed October 13, 2017.

169. Carmine Gallo, "70% Of Your Employees Hate Their Jobs," *Forbes* (November 11, 2011), https://www.forbes.com/sites/

carminegallo/2011/11/11/your-emotionally-disconnected-employees/#5df1eb9542d5, accessed October 10, 2017.

170. Allan Scheweyer, "The Economics of Engagement," *Incentive Research Foundation* (January 5, 2010), http://theirf.org/research/the-economics-of-engagement/206/, accessed October 10, 2017.

171. Jacquelyn Smith, "The Best Workplace Luxuries," *Forbes* (August 24, 2012), https://www.forbes.com/pictures/efkk45jmlg/on-site-massage-chairmassage-therapist/#77d10edc3011, accessed October 13, 2017.

172. Lauren Ufford, "6 Examples of Retail Gamification to Boost Engagement and Sales," *Sales & Marketing* (May 24, 2017), https://www.shopify.com/retail/6-examples-of-retail-gamification-to-boost-engagement-and-sales, accessed October 10, 2017.

173. For this and many other examples, see Kevin Werbech and Dan Hunter, *For the Win: How Game Thinking Can Revolutionize Your Business*, Wharton Digital Press, 2012.

174. Louisa Lim, "China's 'Gold Farmers' Play a Grim Game," *NPR* (May 14, 2007), http://www.npr.org/templates/story/story.php?storyId=10165824, accessed October 13, 2017.

175. Quoted in Jennifer O'Donnell,"Are You a Free-Range or Helicopter Parent?," *verywell* (December 22, 2016), https://www.verywell.com/what-are-helicopter-parents-3288380, accessed October 5, 2017; cf. also Sid Kirchheime, " Overscheduled Child May Lead to a Bored Teen," *WebMD*, https://www.webmd.com/parenting/features/overscheduled-child-may-lead-to-bored-teen#1, accessed October 5, 2017.

176. This section is adapted from Rachel Ashman, Julia Wolny and Michael R. Solomon, "Consuming Self-Regulation in a Technological World," in Michael R. Solomon and Tina M. Lowery, eds., *The Routledge Companion to Consumer Behavior*, London: Taylor & Francis, 2018.

177. Quoted in Neifer, A. "Biohackers are Implanting LED Lights Under Their Skin," *Motherboard (November 9, 2015),* http://motherboard.vice.com/read/biohackers-are-implanting-led-lights-under-their-skin, accessed October 13, 2017.

178. Swan, M. (2013). "The Quantified Self: Fundamental Disruption in Big Data Science and Biological Discovery," *Big Data*, 1(2), 85-99.

179. Fair, J.D., "Physical Culture," *Encyclopedia Brittanica* (August 2, 2016), https://www.britannica.com/topic/physical-culture, accessed October 13, 2017.

180. Gurrin, C., Albatal, R., Joho, H., & Ishi, K., "A Privacy By Design Approach To Lifelogging," in O'Hara et al, (eds.), *Digital Enlightenment: A Handbook*, 2014, IOS Press. 49-61.

181. This chapter is adapted from Michael R. Solomon, *Consumer Behavior: Buying, Having and Being* 12th ed., Hoboken, NJ: Pearson Education, 2016. Cf. also Jagdish N. Sheth and Michael R. Solomon, "Extending the Extended Self in a Digital World," *Journal of Marketing Theory and Practice*, 2014, Volume 22, Number 2: 123-132.

182. Lan Nguyen Chaplin and Deborah Roedder John, "The Development of Self-Brand Connections in Children and Adolescents," *Journal of Consumer Research* 32 (June 2005): 119–129.

183. A. Dwayne Ball and Lori H. Tasaki, "The Role and Measurement of Attachment in Consumer Behavior," *Journal of Consumer Psychology* 1, no. 2 (1992): 155–172.

184. William B. Hansen and Irwin Altman, "Decorating Personal Places: A Descriptive Analysis," *Environment & Behavior* 8 (December 1976): 491–504.

185. Jennifer L. Aaker, "The Malleable Self: The Role of Self-Expression in Persuasion," *Journal of Marketing Research* 36 (February 1999): 45–57; Sak Onkvisit and John Shaw, "Self-Concept and Image Congruence: Some Research and Managerial Implications," *Journal of Consumer Marketing* 4 (Winter 1987): 13–24.

186. Claudia Townsend and Sanjay Sood, "Self-Affirmation Through the Choice of Highly Aesthetic Products," *Journal of Consumer Research* 40, no. 1 (2013): 256–269.

187. Martin Reimann, Raquel Castaño, Judith Zaichkowsky, and Antoine Bechara, "How We Relate to Brands: Psychological and Neurophysiological Insights Into Consumer–Brand Relationships," *Journal of Consumer Psychology* 22, no 1 (2012): 128–142.

188. Quoted in Shirley Y. Y. Cheng, Tiffany Barnett White, and Lan Nguyen Chaplin, "The Effects of Self-brand Connections on Responses to Brand Failure: A New Look at the Consumer–Brand Relationship," *Journal of Consumer Psychology* 22, no. 2 (2012): 280–288.

189. Andrew Adam Newman, "Playing on America's Love for Its 2-Ton Darlings," *New York Times* (December 26, 2013), http://www.nytimes.com/2013/12/27/business/media/playing-on-americas-love-for-its-2-ton-darlings.html, accessed February 24, 2015.

190. C. B. Claiborne and M. Joseph Sirgy, "Self-Image Congruence as a Model of Consumer Attitude Formation and Behavior: A Conceptual Review and Guide for Further Research," paper presented at the Academy of Marketing Science Conference, New Orleans, 1990.

191. Susan Fournier and Julie L. Yao, "Reviving Brand Loyalty: A Reconceptualization within the Framework of Consumer-Brand Relationships," *International Journal of Research in Marketing* 14, no. 5 (December 1997): 451–472; Caryl E. Rusbult, "A Longitudinal Test of the Investment Model: The Development (and Deterioration) of Satisfaction and Commitment in Heterosexual Involvements," *Journal of Personality & Social Psychology* 45, no. 1 (1983): 101–117.

192. Allison R. Johnson, Maggie Matear, and Matthew Thomson, "A Coal in the Heart: Self-Relevance as a Post-Exit Predictor of Consumer Anti-Brand Actions," *Journal of Consumer Research* 38, no. 1 (June 2011): 108–125.

193. A. L. E. Birdwell, "A Study of Influence of Image Congruence on Consumer Choice," *Journal of Business* 41 (January 1964): 76–88; Edward L. Grubb and Gregg Hupp, "Perception of Self, Generalized Stereotypes, and Brand Selection," *Journal of Marketing Research* 5 (February 1986): 58–63.

194. Benedict Carey, "With That Saucy Swagger, She Must Drive a Porsche," *New York Times* (June 13, 2006), www.nytimes.com, accessed March 25, 2015.

195. Ira J. Dolich, "Congruence Relationship Between Self-Image and Product Brands," *Journal of Marketing Research* 6 (February 1969): 80–84; Danny N. Bellenger, Earle Steinberg, and Wilbur W. Stanton, "The Congruence of Store Image and Self Image as It Relates to Store Loyalty," *Journal of Retailing* 52, no. 1 (1976): 17–32; Ronald J. Dornoff and Ronald L. Tatham, "Congruence Between Personal Image and Store Image," *Journal of the Market Research Society* 14, no. 1 (1972): 45–52.

196. www.airnewzealand.com/aboutus/mediacentre/cranial-billboards-campaign.htm, accessed March 5, 2013.

197. https://www.tattoofun.com/blog/custom-temporary-tattoos-fit-marketing-strategy/, accessed December 3, 2017; http://www.staplespromotionalproducts.com/http/wwwstaplespromotionalproductscom/product/1-1/220x201-1/220Temporary20Waterless20Tattoos/80OQX/, accessed December 3, 2017.

198. "The History of Temporary Tattoos," *TemporaryTattoos.com* (May 25, 2013), http://temporarytattoos.com/the-history-of-temporary-tattoos/, accessed March 20, 2015.

199. Gabriel Beltrone, "Woman Gets a Giant Reebok Tattoo, and Her Very Own Ad to Go with It," *Adweek* (September 17, 2014), http://www.adweek.com/adfreak/woman-gets-giant-reebok-tattoo-and-her-very-own-ad-well-160192, accessed March 20, 2015.

200. Scott Smith, Dan Fisher, and S. Jason Cole, "The Lived Meanings of Fanaticism: Understanding the Complex Role of Labels and Categories in Defining the Self in Consumer Culture," *Consumption, Markets & Culture* 10 (June 2007): 77–94.

201. Quoted in Cavan Sieczkowski, "Mariah Carey's Shoe Closet Is Probably Bigger Than Your Apartment," *Huffington Post* (July 20, 2015), http://www.huffingtonpost.com/entry/mariah-careys-shoe-closet-is-probably-bigger-than-your-apartment_55acf41de4b0caf721b322ca, accessed July 21, 2015.

202. Russell W. Belk, "Shoes and Self," *Advances in Consumer Research* (2003): 27–33.

203. Park Ji Kyung and Deborah Roedder John, "Got to Get You into My Life: Do Brand Personalities Rub Off on Consumers?" *Journal of Consumer Research* 37, no. 4 (2010): 655–669.

204. Ernest Beaglehole, *Property: A Study in Social Psychology* (New York: Macmillan, 1932).

205. Adapted from Jagdish N. Sheth and Michael R. Solomon, "Extending the Extended Self in a Digital World," *Journal of Marketing Theory and Practice* 22, no. 2 (2014): 123–132.

206. Russell W. Belk, "Possessions and the Extended Self," *Journal of Consumer Research* 15 (September 1988): 139–168.

207. Robert A. Wicklund and Peter M. Gollwitzer, *Symbolic Self-Completion* (Hillsdale, NJ: Erlbaum, 1982).

208. Cf. https://www.journals.elsevier.com/journal-of-consumer-psychology/forthcoming-articles/the-compensatory-consumer-behavior-model-a-review-of-how-sel, accessed December 3, 2017.

209. Michael R. Solomon and Susan P. Douglas (1987), "Diversity in Product Symbolism: The Case of Female Executive Clothing," *Psychology & Marketing*, 4 (Fall), 189212.

210. Andrew D. Wilson and Sabrina Golonka, "Embodied Cognition Is Not What You Think it Is," *Frontiers in Psychology* (February 12, 2013), http://journal.frontiersin.org/article/10.3389/fpsyg.2013.00058/full, accessed March 19, 2015, doi: 10.3389/fpsyg.2013.00058

211. Sheryl Sandberg, *Lean In: Women, Work, and the Will to Lead*, New York: Random House, 2013, https://www.amazon.com/dp/B009LMTDL0/ref=dp-kindle-redirect?_encoding=UTF8&btkr=1, accessed October 15, 2017.

212. Adam Hajo and Adam D. Galinsky, "Enclothed Cognition," *Journal of Experimental Social Psychology* 48, no. 4 (July 2012): 918–925.

213. Michael R. Solomon (1981), "Dress for Success: Clothing Appropriateness and the Efficacy of Role Behavior," *Dissertation Abstracts International*, 42 (6), Ph.D. Dissertation, Department of Psychology, University of North Carolina at Chapel Hill.

214. Cf. Rachel Ashman, Julia Wolny and Michael R. Solomon, "Consuming Self-Regulation in a Technological World," in Michael R. Solomon and Tina M. Lowery, eds., *The Routledge Companion to Consumer Behavior*, London: Taylor & Francis, 2018.

215. R Y Crist, "Dawn of the Sexbots," *CNET* (August 10, 2017), https://www.cnet.com/news/abyss-creations-ai-sex-robots-headed-to-your-bed-and-heart/, accessed October 15, 2017.

216. Quoted in https://realbotix.systems/, accessed October 15, 2017.

217. Quoted in Ray Kurzweil, "17 Definitions of the Technological Singularity (June 25, 2016), https://www.singularityweblog.com/17-definitions-of-the-technological-singularity/, accessed October 14, 2017.

218. http://Internetofthingsagenda.techtarget.com/definition/thing-in-the-Internet-of-Things, accessed October 14, 2017.

219. This section is adapted from Michael R. Solomon, *Consumer Behavior: Buying, Having and Being* 12th ed., Hoboken, NJ: Pearson Education, 2016.

220. Patricia Cohen, "Oxfam Study Finds Richest 1% is Likely to Control Half of Global Wealth by 2016," *New York Times* (January 19, 2015), http://www.nytimes.com/2015/01/19/business/richest-1-percent-likely-to-control-half-of-global-wealth-by-2016-study-finds.html?smid=nytcore-iphone-share&smprod=nytcore-iphone&_r=1, accessed February 26, 2015.

221. Chris Matthews, "Wealth Inequality in America: It's Worse Than You Think," *Fortune* (October 31, 2014), http://fortune.com/2014/10/31/inequality-wealth-income-us/, accessed April 15, 2015.

222. Bige Saatcioglu and Julie L. Ozanne, "Moral Habitus and Status Negotiation in a Marginalized Working-class Neighborhood," *Journal of Consumer Research* 40, no. 4 (2013): 692–710. cf. also N. Ordabayeva

and P. Chandon, "Getting Ahead of the Joneses: When Equality Increases Conspicuous Consumption Among Bottom-Tier Consumers," *Journal of Consumer Research* 38, no. 10 (2011): 27–41.

223. Elizabeth Holmes, "Luxury Goods Sparkle," *Wall Street Journal* (May 4, 2011), http://professional.wsj.com/article/SB10001424052748703834804576300941315031916.html?mg=reno-secaucus-wsj, accessed June 16, 2011.

224. Dionne Searcey and Robert Gebeloff, "Middle Class Shrinks Further as More Fall Out Instead of Climbing Up," *New York Times* (January 25, 2015), http://www.nytimes.com/2015/01/26/business/economy/middle-class-shrinks-further-as-more-fall-out-instead-of-climbing-up.html?smid=nytcore-iphone-share&smprod=nytcore-iphone&_r=0, accessed February 25, 2015.

225. Gretchen Morgenson, "Despite Federal Regulation, C.E.O.-Worker Pay Gap Data Remains Hidden," *New York Times* (April 10, 2015), http://www.nytimes.com/2015/04/12/business/despite-federal-regulation-ceo-worker-pay-gap-data-remains-hidden.html?ref=business&_r=0, accessed April 14, 2015; Patricia Cohen, "One Company's New Minimum Wage: $70,000 a Year," *New York Times* (April 13, 2015), http://www.nytimes.com/2015/04/14/business/owner-of-gravity-payments-a-credit-card-processor-is-setting-a-new-minimum-wage-70000-a-year.html?ref=business&_r=0, accessed April 14, 2015.

226. Mark Gongloff, "The U.S. Has the Worst Income Inequality in the Developed World, Thanks to Wall Street: Study," *The Huffington Post* (August 15, 2013), http://www.huffingtonpost.com/2013/08/15/income-inequality-wall-street_n_3762422.html, accessed April 14, 2015.

227. Turner, *Sociology: Studying the Human System*, 260.

228. See Ronald Paul Hill and Mark Stamey, "The Homeless in America: An Examination of Possessions and Consumption Behaviors," *Journal of Consumer Research* 17 (December 1990): 303–321; "The Homeless Facts and Figures," NOW (May 2, 2007), www.ask.com/bar?q=What+Percentage+of+Americans+Are+Homeless&page=1&qsrc=6&ab=0&u=http://www.pbs.org/now/shows/305/homeless-facts.html, accessed June 17, 2009.

229. "A Family Affair: Intergenerational Social Mobility Across OECD Countries," *Organization for Economic Co-Operation and Development* (2010), http://www.oecd.org/tax/public-finance/chapter%205%20 gfg%202010.pdf, accessed March 17, 2013; Dan Froomkin, "Social Immobility: Climbing the Economic Ladder Is Harder in the U.S. Than in Most European Countries," *The Huffington Post* (September 21, 2010), http://www.huffingtonpost.com/2010/03/17/social-immobility-climbin_n_501788.html, accessed September 25, 2013.

230. Steve Hargreaves, "The Myth of the American Dream," *CNN Money* (December 9, 2013), http://money.cnn.com/2013/12/09/news/economy/america-economic-mobility/index.html, accessed April 14, 2015.

231. Quoted in "The Partisan Divide on Political Values Grows Even Wider," Pew Research Center (October 5, 2017), http://www.people-press.org/2017/10/05/the-partisan-divide-on-political-values-grows-even-wider/, accessed October 15, 2017.